HUSTLE 'TIL IT HAPPENS

Readers are encouraged to go to www.
MissionPointPress.com to contact the
author or to find information on how to
buy this book in bulk at a discounted rate.

Published by Mission Point Press
2554 Chandler Lake Rd.
Traverse City, MI 49686
(231) 421-9513
www.MissionPointPress.com

ISBN: 978-1-943995-48-6
LoC Control Number: 2017960747

Printed in the United States of America.

HUSTLE

'TIL IT

HAPPENS

TURNING **BOLD DREAMS** INTO **REALITY**

SAM FLAMONT

MISSION POINT PRESS

22 STEPS

CONTENTS

I have three pillars of happiness, and if I begin a journey and realize those pillars cannot be found, I pivot and take another path.

Throughout this book you will see that I have tried, failed, tried again, failed again, and kept pushing forward.

I will never settle for a life that doesn't deliver what I want and need.

As you read this, you will see that the vehicle in which I pursue those pillars has changed, but the vision has never strayed.

Sam Flamont

INTRODUCTION

I want to start this book by asking you a few questions:

→ Where are you now?

→ Are you genuinely happy with where your life is going?

→ Do you start each day with a twinge of regret that you could be doing something more ... perhaps fulfilling a big, bold dream that you set aside a long time ago?

Hustle 'Til It Happens is about being crazy enough, bold enough, brash enough to actually believe in and pursue your dream life with an unrelenting fury. It's a proven program that will get you from where you are now to where you want to go.

This program is not about goal setting alone, but the **big idea** is to **DREAM BOLD** when it comes to setting your sights on your dream.

I use the term "**bold**" for a few reasons, but the main reason is that I want you to courageously reach for goals so high that even if you come up short you can still be really good, or even great. These are the goals that require massive action and the courage to face failure, but have a chance to dramatically change your life.

A bold, or what some people call an unrealistic goal, is not truly unrealistic. It's more likely to be improbable or extremely difficult to reach. The only goal that I deem truly unrealistic is for a human to fly without assistance — gravity will win every time. But that's it. The rest of the world's possibilities are open to you.

To be clear, the **Hustle 'Til It Happens** program is not just a goal-setting practice. It includes goal setting, but it's actually part of an entire process that includes setting specific and extremely lofty goals, creating a process to achieve them, understanding your "why" (your motivation), then taking proper action with the proper mind set.

The theory of **Hustle 'Til It Happens** is

→ if it has been done before, you can do it

→ and just because it hasn't been done before, doesn't mean it's impossible for you to achieve

As a performance coach, I used the **Hustle 'Til It Happens** program to help all kinds of people: Young men and women full of ambition, just starting their journey. Middle-age folks who were stuck and wanted more out of life. Some of my clients were people who'd succumbed to the everyday grind and were looking to reignite the fire — to get back to living the life they'd once intended.

The **Hustle 'Til It Happens** program revolves around two principles. First, it's about going all-out with a specific plan to achieve your goal. Second, it's learning to ignore those who tell you that it's unrealistic to live your dream life, who insist that you be realistic or "settle" for average.

What do I mean by "average"? Basically, average is settling or accepting less than you deserve out of life because you are not willing to push through adversity in order to live your dream. Average has nothing to do with how much money you have, or how many toys you can buy, or what level you're at in a company. Being average comes down to settling for a life that's not making you happy.

Before I introduce you to my **Hustle 'Til It Happens** program, I would first like to tell you the stories of some real-life people who have used the program to get from where they were to where they want to be.

Mike: Getting Unstuck from a Bad Career Choice

Mike is a guy with a job. Although he had the title of manager, he basically sold pretzels and chips to stores across Michigan. Mike hated it. The hours were long and his boss was crude and disrespectful to him. Mike was in his 40s and felt stuck, due to past decisions that did not allow him to move forward professionally. But before you think that he was unhappy, let me explain that he was far from it. His daughters and wife always brought a smile to his face and he often talked about them with affection and love.

Mike is what some would call the "average American citizen," but I would call him anything but average. Why? Because his work ethic is unbelievable. Although he had a job he only tolerated, he worked as though he owned the company. He was (and still is) a person who cannot easily sit still: If there is a task he sets out to do, he gets it done and done very well. He has a strong desire to learn and improve his life. But in his "manager" job, there was nowhere for him to go. With each passing day, the pain of remaining the same was starting to hurt more than the pain and discomfort of change. Mike had no interest in starting a business or being his own boss — what he wanted is what almost everyone I come in contact with wants: the ability to grow in his career.

One day, Mike decided enough was finally enough and he enrolled in classes at Henry Ford Community College. Here was a guy balancing a real life, not the typical carefree college student. He had a full-time job (50-60 hours per week), a family, housework, and the other obligations each of us juggle on a daily basis. But Mike made the leap.

As time went by, he earned A after A after A. He had to put in serious work — getting up at 4 a.m. and working at night after his kids went to bed — but he dominated all of his classes and finished his associate's degree with a 4.0 grade point average. He then searched for a four-year school to earn his bachelor's degree, but quickly realized he couldn't afford the tuition. Still, he kept applying in order to keep his momentum. He was accepted into most all of them, but when he saw the tuition costs, he'd lose hope.

One day, Mike received great news. He got a letter from Wayne State University informing him that he was welcome to attend their college and finish his degree *at no cost*. Yes, he received a full ride! To help pay the bills at home, he took a co-op job through the college, even though it meant a massive pay cut. His family got behind him, and Mike put 100 percent into his minimum wage job. Early on, for example, he designed a spreadsheet that saved his boss six hours of work every Monday. Mike proved he was a valuable addition, and after he graduated he found a new job that he loves.

Now this is where you jump in and say, "Oh, he was really lucky" or "That hardly ever happens." Although I would agree with the latter, the former is an excuse made by people who are afraid to take action.

Let's Investigate How Mike Got "Lucky"

First, he was willing to step out of his comfort zone.

Second, he set a goal.

Third, he created a process to reach that goal.

Fourth, he worked his butt off on a daily basis, understanding it was going to be hard for a few years, but that the rest of his life would be better for it.

Lastly, he was unrealistic enough to believe two things: he really could do all of these things *and* he really did deserve everything he wanted in life.

Thinking that you deserve what you want in life **is not** unrealistic.

I always tell people, "You deserve what you want, but you will only get what you earn." Mike earned his new life, and he truly deserves it. Throughout his journey, Mike used every step of the **Hustle 'Til It Happens** program to get from stuck, to unstuck, to being fulfilled in his career.

This is what the **Hustle 'Til It Happens** program is all about. You will hear stories of people with monster dreams, dreams of heading up a car company, of becoming an entrepreneur, or getting into professional baseball (that's my own). You will also hear how people applied this program to create fulfillment in their current career or relationship. The **Hustle 'Til It Happens** program isn't just for people who want to chase a huge dream — it's also for those who want to live a particular lifestyle.

Big Goals, No Regrets

Some people think it is unrealistic to strive for a big goal. I am not that someone. As soon as I set out to play baseball in the big leagues, many people told me to get a back-up plan, to stay in school, and to be a realistic kid. I never let it bother me. I wanted to be one of the 750 people in the world to play in the major leagues and, after all, if 750 people were already in the big leagues, my goal wasn't so much unrealistic as it was bold.

I always knew the challenge ahead of me was highly improbable, but I loved that. I didn't want a guarantee, I just wanted a shot, and I wanted to earn that shot. I was chasing a dream and that's why I worked harder than anyone around me every step of the way. My work ethic matched my goal. While others kids my age were hanging out with friends, I was in the weight room. While they were out getting drunk, I was busting my butt. While they were playing video games, I was visualizing and planning for my success. I wanted to look back, regardless of the outcome, and say, "I did everything I could have, and in the end I was either good enough to make it or

I was not." As I am writing this, I know that I put in my maximum effort, and that's why I have zero regrets looking back.

Throughout this book you will read about people I have worked with directly to achieve their dreams. I also write about people I've studied or interviewed regarding their journeys. Some of these people are famous — you'll recognize their names and achievements. Others you won't know, and may never know, but they have all implemented the **Hustle 'Til It Happens** program in order to achieve goals and live an intended life. The good news is that as a performance coach, I've seen people change from skepticism to a deeply entrenched belief that their dreams are not only *going* to happen or *might* happen, but instead, they *are* happening.

Ed: The Magical Ring Finder

Ed Walker is a successful businessman in the greater Detroit area. Ed owned a company named "W Enterprise," a manufacturer of a wide range of products for the auto and aerospace industries. When the economic crash hit in 2008 and the auto industry struggled to survive, Ed's business felt the impact in the worst way. Casually, he talked as if his business was running as smoothly and as profitably as ever, but in no way was he naïve about the future. The way he explained it to me, he was leading with confidence simply because he knew it was the *only way* to lead if his business had any chance of succeeding. Eventually a large automotive company came in and performed what is known as a hostile takeover, paying Ed much less than he wanted for his company. Failure, right? Wrong.

Over the next few years, Ed went to work building a new business. He was able to retain many of his same contacts because of his reputation for honesty and delivering work at the highest standard, even though the new business was in a different sector. He even kept a few of the same employees. More importantly, Ed just kept putting one foot in front of the other and was eternally optimistic about the future. He lived as though his dreams and goals were actually happening, and that is why he was able to rebound.

In a crazy turn of events, the company that took over his first business ended up going bankrupt and, like all entrepreneurs, Ed saw an opportunity to start over. It wasn't an overnight success story — he knew he needed to streamline and scale back, plus the bankrupted company had stranded scores of clients. But slowly and surely, Ed started to see the light of success, and occasionally he saw it burn out again. But he remained confident that his company was going to make it, and because of his attitude, he was able to keep working hard and make the required moves to help the company succeed. Had he at any point stopped believing, the company would have failed.

Ed's eternal optimism brought his company a long way, and he now feels as though he is on solid ground. He's enjoying the growth and earnings of the business, but he's not sitting on his hands. Like most high achievers, once Ed reaches a goal, he sets another bold and unrealistic goal.

You may be wondering why this story is titled The Magical Ring Finder when it's about a businessman and his triumphs. It's because Ed put into practice his unrealistic goal-setting one evening in Indian River, Michigan. I was with Ed and a bunch of our friends playing a game of touch football. As I dropped back to throw what would become a touchdown pass, my cousin Derek jumped to block it. As he jumped, he swung his hand toward the ball, and when he landed, he yelled, "Oh #!!*." Derek had lost his wedding ring.

A ring is hard enough to find in the first place, but the darkness and three inches of snow made the probability of success swing to the far side of unrealistic. We made a plan and followed it to the letter. First, we spread out and began drawing a grid in order to check off the areas that we had already covered. We did this for over an hour, but came up with nothing. Next, we decided to call a neighbor who owned a metal detector. *Great*, was our collective thought. *This ring is all but found!* But after another hour of digging, we got nothing.

When we decided to call it quits, Derek walked into the house visibly upset. This is when Ed approached him and calmly said, "We will find it in the morning."

The next day, I had to head home to Traverse City, but on the drive I called to ask how the search was going. Derek happily told me that Ed had found the ring that morning in about ten minutes, and now they were all back inside enjoying coffee.

The take-home is Ed's mindset: there was never any doubt in Ed's mind that the ring would be found, just as there were never any doubts that his business goals and dreams were happening. Ed's mindset allowed him to overcome adversity and start another company that is now doing more than $40 million in sales and is still growing. Ed has been called lucky, stupid, smart, unrealistic, and more, but through it all, he simply set a goal, created a process, and stayed consistent, persistent, and patient. Because of these attributes Ed found success where it looked like none existed.

Jeff: All the Way to Omaha

Cleveland Indians draft pick Jeff Opalewski has a story that resonates due to the fact that he was once overcome by the negativity of being told that he had to be *realistic*. When I asked him if he ever tells people to tone down their dreams and "be realistic," he replied, "Years ago I did, before I was able to develop the mentality I currently have. I would never do that now." Jeff was extremely candid and open in our interview, saying, "I was a skinny, self-conscious kid who had a poor self-image and low self-confidence … until I started throwing a baseball ninety miles an hour as a senior in high school. That, of course, gave me permission to turn into an arrogant jerk — that still had low self-confidence — but now I was masking it by making others feel worse about themselves."

Even as Jeff began to throw a ball as hard as the big league pitchers, there were still a lot of people who decided it was their place to tell him what he could and could not achieve. This had a detrimental effect on him, as he explains: "I've been told to be realistic my entire life and, unfortunately, I conformed for a long time. Enough people told me to be realistic about pitching in the big leagues that I allowed a seed of doubt to be planted in my mind."

Jeff further explained that hundreds of humbling events during his college career as a baseball player led him to a crossroads that required that he make a choice about who he really was. " I decided to pursue a career in coaching. Admittedly, initially, it was for my own ego. I wanted to have a positive impact on thirty-five young men every year and aid in their maturation process, preparing them to be men once their time in college is through."

Jeff's self-awareness and personal accountability reflect the very reason he was able to grow and move forward with confidence. Yet he still has to deal with the naysayers. People still look at him and tell him — non-verbally — to be realistic when he declares that Central Michigan University players will earn their way to Omaha, home of the college baseball world series. One sure thing is that Jeff has grown in such a way that there is no seed of doubt when it comes to his belief that Central Michigan *will* get to Omaha. Some people might call that a little bold, but seeing how schools from the same conference have been there, there's nothing unrealistic about it. Sure, it will be extremely difficult, but do not confuse that with "unrealistic" — unless, of course, you don't plan to work as hard as needed.

Jeff talked to me about the "Separator Trait" — the ability to push beyond your comfort zone and challenge yourself to find out what you are capable of. "A lot of people are capable of doing what they want," he explained, "but most are not capable of doing what they need to in order to be in that position." I could not agree more. This kind of challenge speaks to mental toughness, creating and working through your process, and simply going after what you want until it becomes yours — all of which I will cover in this book.

Anthony: Aiming for the top ...
of Ford Motor Company

I was talking to a group of student athletes from Northwood University in Midland, Michigan, when a young man began to tell me the story of his teammate, Anthony DiPaolo. Like all students at Northwood, Anthony was a business major, but he did not subscribe to the idea of simply falling in line and taking what was given. Anthony was looking for an internship, but he had no intention of becoming a normal coffee-fetcher and paperwork intern. He wanted more, and he knew he would have to ask for more in order to get it.

So that's what he did. Anthony sat down at his computer and began writing a letter to the president of Ford Motor Company. Anthony asked for an internship, but told the president that he did not want to be a normal intern — he wanted to learn how to be the president of Ford Motor Company. He went even further, explaining that he wanted the job of the man he was writing the letter to after he retired.

Although his friends thought he was crazy, a little while later Anthony received a response and an offer to be an intern at Ford … and to rest assured that he was not going to be a "normal intern." Instead, he was going to be working with high-level executives who pull the trigger on big deals. Anthony accepted the position and started the internship after the school year ended, but this story is not over. While he interned at Ford, he took the lead on a few projects, including one that was extremely profitable to Ford. His work earned him a promised job offer after he graduates, a level or two above an entry-level position.

Anthony's story started with the bold expectation that the president would receive the letter, actually read it, and take it seriously. But it wasn't so bold after all, because that's exactly what happened, and Anthony's life is better for it.

Why Didn't I Ever Try?

Of course, being bold, or even unrealistic, opens you up to ridicule, second-guessing, and doubt. Of course, there's always the risk of failure. But when failure happens, I guarantee that you are on the right track. People who spread hate and self-doubt are simply trying to make you stop ... just in case you succeed. Because if you did succeed, it would mean *they* would have to look back on their own lives and say, "Why didn't I ever try?"

> People want to stop you from pursuing your dreams because they are too lazy and scared to pursue their own.

When Roger Bannister was striving to run a four-minute mile, everyone said he was crazy, that it was not humanly possible, and dangerous, to boot. His answer was to *keep trying, keep training, and keep believing.* Roger Bannister broke the four-minute mile on May 6, 1954, proving that what was once thought to be bold and unrealistic was only extremely difficult.

In the exact same year, John Landy ran a sub-four-minute mile and actually beat Bannister's time. The feat had gone from impossible, to two times in one year, to now being the standard in which a miler is judged.

Once Bannister broke the record, it gave people hope — not only hope that they could break the four-minute mile, but the belief they could run even quicker, and that is what they did. Instead of waiting for permission, these bold dreamers went out and set the tone.

> Being **bold** proves that your goal is hard, but not impossible.

Will Smith once said, "Being realistic is the most common path to mediocrity." Take that quote and examine the world around you. Think about the things you see — or even touch — and ask yourself if they were once considered unrealistic. Flip on a light switch, send an email, or fly in a plane 37,000 feet above the ground. The best way to stay average is to start with an average goal. Like that plane in the sky, you'll need to be **bold** and aim high.

PART I: DEFINE YOUR GOALS

MY OWN STORY

THE NIGHT THAT CHANGED MY LIFE

It was a typical Tuesday night in Lexington, Kentucky, in 1993. I was at a friend's house playing basketball when his mom called him in for dinner and told me it was time to go home. I turned away and walked up the hill to my house — a long, lonely walk that often ended with finding my mother drunk, high on pills, or both.

I dreaded this walk, which is why I often stayed away as long as possible. On this particular night, it was even worse than normal. I walked in through the garage door, left my stuff in the mudroom, took the right turn through the doorway that led to the stairs, and saw my mom lying motionless on the floor.

It was obvious what had happened — she had passed out and fallen down an entire flight of steps. Fruit Loops and spilled milk lined the wall from the very top step all the way to the bottom. A bowl and spoon lay next to her body. I could see that she was still breathing because her chest was expanding, but I lost it. I broke down crying and ran outside. I grabbed my bike and rode back and forth in front of my house in the dark, waiting for my stepfather, Chuck, to return home from work.

When Chuck pulled into the driveway, he saw I was shaken up and asked what the problem was. All I could tell him, between sobs, was, "You'll see." When Chuck saw my mom crumpled on the floor, he shook his head in utter disbelief.

At this point in my life, Chuck and my mother were in the middle of an awful divorce and, although they were still in the same house,

Chuck slept upstairs and my mom downstairs. So what happened next completely floored me — Chuck bent down and tenderly checked my mom to make sure she was okay. Then he picked up the cereal bowl and walked up the stairs, picking up each Fruit Loop along the way. He put the cereal in the garbage, the spoon and bowl in the sink, then grabbed a towel and began cleaning up the milk. After that was done, he picked up my still unconscious mom and got her in bed. After he'd tucked her in, he turned his attention to me. He helped me get ready for bed, too, gave me a kiss, and tucked me in.

This story was the major turning point in my life. It made me realize that we are in full control of our own happiness. We are also in full control of the decisions we make.

People often say, "You made me do it," but in reality, everyone has a choice to make the right — or wrong — decision. In the above scenario, Chuck made a decision that impacted my life in a profound manner. First of all, he never mentioned a word about the incident to my mom, at least not in my presence. And most importantly, no matter how many awful things she did or said to him, he never responded with hate.

What I realized was that Chuck lived by a strong value system and always tried to do the right thing. Nothing could throw him off balance — not my mother's drinking, not her profanity, not her vindictive actions. I will discuss this concept further along in the book, but I want to point out that Chuck was a very successful businessman with wonderful relationships. His mindset was the major reason why.

I believe I was fortunate in my upbringing. I believe that all the negativity I witnessed — the drugs, alcohol, prison time, fist fights, arguments, divorces, and teen pregnancies — actually *helped* me because I saw what life would be like if I decided to make the same choices that the people around me had made. Just as importantly, my stepfather proved to me that I had the *power of choice*.

I was born in Dearborn Heights, Michigan and raised by parents who never married. My mother was hardly ever home — she worked three different jobs at a time, all as a waitress. I would often come home to my mom passed out on the couch from a combination of pills and alcohol. She would occasionally wake up to swear at me and tell me I was worthless, a liar, and that I'd be nothing in life — that I'd turn out just like my brother. She used the f-word as an adjective, noun, and verb in just about every sentence that came out of her mouth.

My brother used to steal my bike to buy drugs. He'd also take me to the store to show me how he stole gum and other things so he could take them to school and make money. He'd then turn around and use the money to buy drugs. This same brother went to prison at the age of seventeen, and to this day has spent twenty-plus years of his life behind bars on charges that range from breaking and entering to accessory to murder.

Both my parents have issues with alcohol, and when I was a kid, my mom was drug-addicted as well. I have an aunt who spent time in prison for murdering her husband.

I spent summers with my dad, but he wasn't there to protect me during the school year. He was a carpet layer who worked long hours and drank everyday as well. This was hard to watch, especially given the history of my mom, but the difference between my dad and my mom was substantial. My dad, although he would drink a lot and sometimes pass out on the couch, was always there. He was always supportive. I always felt like he was my biggest fan. He was at games and he spoke to me like a human being. He's not perfect — neither am I — but to me, he is wonderful. I love my father and everything he is.

My mom married Chuck when I was four years old. She probably thought she'd be on Easy Street since he earned a good income. But when she quit her waitressing jobs, she went downhill fast. I've already described to you our fun-filled nights. When I didn't think things could get any worse, my mom divorced Chuck and took up with a new man. Suddenly, in the middle of my eighth grade year, she announced we were moving down to Florida. She put in me in a U-Haul for the 1,500-mile trip with a friend of her boyfriend. He reeked of cigarette smoke, body odor, and cheap beer. I'd finally had enough. Shortly after we moved into the Florida house, I returned to my dad's home back in Michigan and didn't speak to my mom for years.

I Deserve More

I knew from an early age that I wanted more, but most importantly, I knew I *deserved* more. I set my mind to making my life better than what I saw and experienced on a daily basis. Everything I have accomplished in life and everything I am doing today started with that one thought. *I deserve more.*

I believe that my painful upbringing made my will stronger and allowed me to outlast opponents and dig deep in stressful situations. I could have used my childhood as an excuse to give up, fail, to go down the same path as my mom and brother and aunt. Instead, every time I saw something negative, I created a positive spin with my thoughts. When I saw my mom passed-out drunk, I thought to myself, *How am I going to be a better parent?* Not only did I think that, but I actually formulated plans in my head. I vowed that there would be no getting drunk in front of my kids, no swearing at them, and no yelling. I was going to treat them with respect and "walk the talk" as a positive role model. I created a world in my mind, a world far different than the world I lived in. This wasn't a fantasy. I was not trying to escape reality. Rather, I was creating a plan for the future that gave me hope.

This planning started around the age of twelve, when I really began to notice the negative things in my everyday surroundings. When I truly comprehended what was going on, I began to strategize about how I was going to live better. I knew that nobody should be treated the way my mom was treating me, just as I knew how wrong it was that my ninth grade brother took me — a fourth grader — to stores to teach me how to steal. I never wanted to be like *anyone* in my family, not even my father. I wanted to be *me*. I wanted to carve my own path, because the paths that were in front of me on a daily basis did not make anyone happy. This may sound like I felt that I was better than the people around me, but it wasn't that — I simply believed *I deserved more* and I knew *I'd never get more* if I did the things they did.

We Become What Occupies Our Thoughts

My thoughts began to dominate my world. I imagined how to create a different scenario for my own life. I used to carry a journal and write each thought down. From the age of ten, I mostly thought about playing major league baseball, being successful, and making a ton of money. Everyone would want my autograph! I would talk to myself on the walk home from school and think about how I would be on television someday. I would set up TV interviews with my stuffed animals (they were famous TV hosts) and they'd ask me about the game that day and how I'd won it with a walk-off home run.

By the time I was twenty-two, these thoughts and dreams changed a bit. But back when I was ten, I was fixated on becoming like Alan Trammell. I wanted to play in Tiger Stadium, and since I was able to use my thoughts to create my world, I would put myself in Tiger Stadium on a nightly basis. I had other thoughts, but they were passing thoughts — some good, some very dark, but they flowed right on by. The only *real* thought that stuck in my head was playing professional baseball — I was consumed by it.

I had no idea what it would take to get where I wanted to go, but I did know who I wanted to be. I talked about it to grown-ups, friends, teachers, my mom (before she began heavily drinking) — anybody who asked me about my goals. It was the only thing I wanted in life and, as I grew older, the thoughts became stronger. The more I learned about the massive effort required, the more focused and intense my thoughts became.

> My dream started with a simple thought, and that simple thought took hold of my soul. That thought created a fire that nobody could put out. It created a direction in my life and gave me a mission. It made my life worth living and gave me a sense of being in control of my destiny.

My thought took shape as a goal, and the goal became a process of actions. It required that I be consistent, persistent, and patient. This experience made me a firm believer that we are not a product of our environment, rather that we are a product of our *thoughts*. We become what occupies our thoughts.

I also believe that while everything starts with a thought, we must take those thoughts to the next level. To that end, I've created a very detailed process that allows me to do just that. It's a process that helps me stay focused and allows me to see daily successes as they happen. Because I see daily successes, I am continually encouraged to keep going. This process worked for me and others who achieved — or are in the process of achieving — unique dreams. It will also work for you.

STEP 1: LISTEN TO YOUR THOUGHTS

The **Hustle 'Til It Happens** program begins with a thought. Your daily, unbidden thoughts will lead you to the next step of creating your vision of success.

Exercise:

What actionable thoughts that could help you live a positive life are you ignoring? Fill in this sentence:

If I took this step: _____ my life would become better.

WHAT DOES SUCCESS MEAN TO YOU?

I firmly believe that success is living life *exactly as you intend it*. By defining success this way, you can assume power over your future. Your definition will give you the confidence and purpose you need to move forward. When you assume decision-making power over your future, you gain a sense of strength, and you'll need this strength to go forward with certainty and conviction.

I believe in huge, unrealistic dreams, but that doesn't mean you have to let me or anyone else decide what your dream is. In order to succeed, you must define your *own* success. Maybe it's living on a sailboat in Jamaica. Maybe it's starting your own restaurant. Perhaps it's earning $500,000 a year so you can do whatever the heck you want *and* save for your kids' college and retirement. It's *your* dream.

> Now is the time to close your eyes and imagine exactly what your dream looks like. This is where you get to define your success and take control of your life and journey.

Some of you are just starting out, while others are trying to regain your dream and get back on track. For the latter, this can be tough, but it can also be energizing because you're probably wondering if your original path is still the right one. If it isn't, what is? Rest assured that you can still set your path — you don't need to be young — but it will take a lot of work. *Believe that your dreams are worth it.*

For those of you who are just starting out, remember to take firm control of your dream and ignore friends or family members who tell you to "be realistic" or that "you're crazy" or "it won't work out" or — my least favorite of all — "to get a back-up plan."

In the **Hustle 'Til It Happens** program, it's all about setting goals so high that if you hit them, you are one of the best, and if you miss them, you can still be really good or even great.

The most important part of the program is not the goal itself, but the process you create and the intention in which you go about your daily life.

A Goal Is Not an End

I don't define success as reaching a defined goal. Why? Because reaching a goal means it is time to set a new one. I believe true success is **living the life you intend to live.**

I have never changed my vision of what I wanted my life to look like, but I've often changed the vehicle. The thing to remember is, *if what you are doing is no longer serving you, it's okay to change.*

You may find yourself unwilling to pivot or change direction because you feel like you are quitting. But it isn't quitting, it's actually becoming self-aware. It's a rare — **bold** — person who can say, "I'm making good money at my job, growing my business, growing my savings account, but it just isn't what I want to be doing on a daily basis and therefore it is time to find my dream life."

In my story, I made it to the minor leagues, but came up short of the big leagues. Even so, I still consider that a rare achievement. The fact is, less than one percent of the baseball population ever makes it to the minor leagues. Plus, my quest set me up for the success I am now having as a real estate agent and real estate investor. Why? Because along the way I faced adversity on a regular basis and I always drew on my work ethic and determination to continue towards my goals.

In my journey to get into the big leagues, I realized that at the end of the day, somebody would still always be in charge of me, and that taught me a bigger lesson — I wanted freedom. I realized that just because I came up short of a goal, that didn't mean I hadn't come out on top. Actually, it was because I came up short of a goal that I wrote this book, spent time delivering motivational speeches, sold CDs, worked as a performance coach for people who wanted to change their lives, and was able to become a successful real estate agent in my first year. I came out on top because failing to make the big leagues taught me how to overcome adversity. I had the strength and conviction to move forward and find success on my own terms — to achieve the freedom that I wanted. My persistence in pursuing this freedom allowed me to obtain it.

> I firmly believe that most people are physically capable of achieving their highest goals, but they are not mentally strong enough. Their belief level is not nearly high enough to continue to persist when all hope seems lost. Persistence is the key to success.

When I began in real estate, I set a goal to own 100 rental units. I knew that in order to do that, I needed to start quickly. In my first year as a real estate agent — one in which I was down to my last $1,500 before my first closing — I ended up owning 11 rental units. How did that happen? Because I do not fear losing my money, *I fear not living the life I want to live.*

Those first rentals put me in a bind financially, but I knew that in the long-term, the short-term pain would be worth it. My entire life has taught me to suffer a little now for a big win later. I was not afraid to spend almost all of my money on rental buildings because my work ethic told me I would earn that money back and be okay. I do not value money for material things, I value money for the options and choices it gives me. I want to be free, have fun, give back, and make money, At the age of 37, I'm doing all of those.

The Paths to Success

Defining success will take some work because it's not actually setting a goal — it's painting a picture of your future life. There can be many different paths to success, and those are **goals**.

For example, after I left baseball, I opened up my own indoor baseball facility in order to be my own boss and get the freedom I wanted. Although I was helping a lot of people, I quickly realized that *freedom* wasn't part of the package. I owned a business but, in reality, I owned a job. I had absolutely no choice but to be there and to work fifty hours a week. It didn't matter that I owned the business — what mattered was that I had lost my freedom.

This is how I ended up walking away from the business and handing it over to my partner. The business was his, free and clear. He did a nice job with it, too. He actually grew it, but was forced to work more and more and more — and that is exactly what I saw coming. I had to escape. In some people's minds, this was a failure on my part. But I saw staying as a failure — that business was a time trap. It would never have allowed me to achieve my true definition of success.

VISION OF SUCCESS

That business was, at first, a path to my definition of success. But at the end of the day, it was not the right path. I regrouped and took time to redefine what success meant for me.

I realized that part of it was helping others succeed.

I also wanted the freedom each day to call my own shots — I call it "time freedom."

Of course, I also wanted to make enough money to have fun.

Be Specific

After outlining this vision of success, I created a process to achieve it. This required some careful thinking. For example, my wish to help people was pretty broad, so I defined it more specifically as "reducing the time it takes people to reach their goal, help them overcome fear, find their true passion and dream, and give them confidence to proceed with certainty." I honestly want to help people make their lives better, however my skill set allows.

My definition of *time freedom* has to do with my day — what puts me ahead and what makes me happy. I am typing this from my home office, but sometimes I work out of a coffee shop. Other days I may choose not to do any actual work at all and head to the golf course or to Chicago to visit friends. I use time to read, exercise, think, work, and spend meaningful time with my family. I am not filthy stinking rich, but that was never a goal. My goal is do meaningful work and to have enough money not to worry about money, to invest for the future, and to do what I want. Money doesn't buy happiness, but not having money buys nothing.

There are a lot of people who, like me, would like to take a computer and work wherever they want in the world — California, Spain, Mexico. The freedom to work when and where you want is a huge benefit in my book. As a real estate agent, people think I am tied to the business, that my life revolves around my phone and email. Sure, I get a lot of calls and emails but I still have freedom, and I have that freedom because I set up my real estate career in such a way that it will enrich my life, not take over my life. This happened because my path going into real estate had a clear direction and an exact purpose. I imagined how I wanted to run my business and I achieved that vision. I'm convinced that clearly defining "success" and setting goals is one of the reasons that I'm successful.

Notice, again, that I'm not defining success solely based on money. Although I have money and am steadily building my business, high earnings were never my sole ambition. Instead, my goal was *to trade value for money*. As I see it, the more people I help, the more money I make, so I put my focus on helping people by adding value to their lives.

Let me spell out exactly how this is working for me. My present goal is to sell 101 homes a year. That sales goal also means helping dozens of individuals, couples, and families find homes that fit their needs and their budgets. I also have a goal of helping my investor, builder, and flipper clients make $1,000,000 a year. Sure, this nearly impossible goal benefits me as well, but it also makes me dig deep for deals that aren't obvious. It's not just about selling them a house, it's about making the right "value" moves for them. By focusing on "value," I can make money and stay true to my mission of helping others. For example, if I can't see my clients reaching the necessary return on their investment, I don't pitch them the house. Also, I might spend time researching potential home purchases for hours, only to find that none of them work. That's okay — that's my job and that's how I bring value to others.

STEP 2: DEFINE YOUR SUCCESS

It's time for you to begin to define, or redefine your success.

Sit down and paint your future picture. Ask yourself: What do you want out of this life? What do you see yourself being able to do? Note that it's okay to say you want to be filthy stinking rich, if that is the case. There's no judgment here. This is your success, so create it and own it.

As you start painting pictures and asking questions, you may realize that some of the things you once thought you wanted to do no longer line up with your new definition. Narrowing your vision is vital to getting to the nitty-gritty of the specific paths you can take. It's the first and most necessary step in setting your ultimate goal.

So take your time. Dig deep into your psyche. Maybe you're not conscious of a vision — maybe you've been too afraid to dream because the challenges of life have overwhelmed you. You may realize, like I did, that your success comes down to an emotion, or feeling, and not a tangible thing. Any of this is fine because, again, this is **your** success. Have fun on this journey — it will be the most rewarding expedition of your life.

EXPLORE WHERE YOU ARE NOW AND HOW THE #!!% YOU GOT THERE

The reason we set a specific goal is to give us a *destination*. I love the quote by Lewis Carroll that says, "If you don't know where you are going, any road will do." But when you have a goal, you have a destination.

Now, the first thing to do in getting to where you want to go is to locate where you are in life *right now*. Setting the goal is like a GPS. Some people think a GPS only finds your end destination, while others don't really give it any thought at all — they just plug in the destination and follow the directions. The thing about GPS is that it *must first find out where you are*. Once it locates you, it then can give you the road map to get you where you want to be. Likewise, to reach your destination, you must first do an inventory of where you are in life.

This exercise will give you a time-line perspective of what needs to be done from this point forward in order to reach your final destination.

STEP 3: FACE THE MUSIC

This is an exercise I provided my clients in our weekly calls. Remember to write down your answers and be honest.

Ask yourself two extremely important questions. They will be tough to answer, but you'll need to answer them thoroughly and honestly before you can move forward. This step will create accountability and the answers will set you free and allow you to move forward with confidence.

1. What got you here? What in your life has got you to this point? What or who gets the blame?

2. What is keeping you here?

Write down everything that's slowing you down, no matter how irrelevant it may appear.

What Now?

Take a close look at what you wrote for the first question. Did you blame your stuckness on job loss, divorce, lack of money, or lack of resources? Although all the above may be real, and even painful, the simple fact is you must move forward to get forward. A job loss is an opportunity to create, a divorce is an opportunity to gain understanding.

I'm not saying a divorce or a job loss should not affect you, but I am saying that at some point, and hopefully soon, you must get over the bad stuff if you plan to move forward.

A lack of money, of technology, or access to a car is also real but, again, it's also something you must overcome. *These are roadblocks, not dead ends.* These are examples of adversity, not examples of the way your life must and will play out. You need to toughen up and get to the real reason why you're stuck.

A first step is to accept where you are in life and how you got there. One of the greatest detractors of our success is to wallow in missed opportunities. Deep regret will even paralyze some people. There is no time for that. Like the country singer Vince Gill says, "There ain't no future in the past." Or like Jay-Z says, "You gotta learn to live with regrets." No matter what version you prefer, the idea is the same: *it's time to accept the things you have not done and the time you spent not doing them.*

A second step is to not feel overwhelmed. It's easy to feel crushed even before you get started by thinking about how much time it will take to reach a goal, particularly if it involves getting a college degree or starting a new career from square one. Put it out of your mind — no matter what you do, time will pass anyway. Time continues to move even if you don't. The only question is, will you have accomplished what you wanted or will you kick yourself for never having started?

> We must accept where we are at, let go of any regrets we have, and stay away from any thoughts about the time it will take. We must immerse ourselves in the moment, and then start moving forward from where we are.

WRITE YOUR GOALS DOWN AND FIND A FRIEND

Now that we're in the moment, we must focus all of our attention on the goal we have set. From here on out, we're going to get into the exact process of setting our goals and keeping track of our progress.

Make Your Goal Come Alive

When a thought keeps nagging at you, it's begging you to pay attention to it. It is literally *begging* you to create a goal to bring it to life. For me, the thought of playing in major league baseball would not leave me, but I never really knew about goal-setting until tenth grade. That's when a speaker came to our school and encouraged us to write our goals down.

This speaker told us the story of Jim Abbott. Abbott was a pitcher in the big leagues, and he had only one fully functional arm. When he pitched, he would rest his glove on his stump, throw the pitch, then quickly put the glove on his hand. I was truly inspired to hear about a guy with such a great disadvantage who not only successfully reached the big leagues, but *dominated* the game.

The speaker told us that Jim Abbott wrote down on a note card that he was going to pitch in the big leagues for the New York Yankees. When I heard that, it was over. I was definitely writing my goal down. I can honestly say that I don't remember much of what the speaker said after that story because all I could focus on was getting home, writing my goal on a note card, and hanging it above my bed.

So it began: the ritual of writing my goals down and making them come alive started that day. I went straight home, got a note card out of a drawer, pulled out a pen and wrote, "I will play shortstop for the Detroit Tigers in the major leagues." As soon as I wrote it down, I hung it right above my pillow. I looked at it for a few minutes while imagining suiting up with the Tigers and feeling my first step onto the field in front of all those fans. I took everything in and I became excited. Although in the past, I would *tell* people about my goal of playing baseball, I now had it *written down* and it was specific.

STEP 4: WRITE IT DOWN

I encourage you to write down your ultimate goal and place it somewhere you can see it **every day**. The reason for this is that it creates accountability and excitement.

Having your goal written down and looking at it daily will create excitement because it will force you to think about achieving that goal and, in turn, you can begin to feel what accomplishing an unrealistic goal feels like.

My note card went with me every step of the way. After high school it was on my wall in my apartment at Grand Rapids Community College, and then when I went to Western Michigan University. The crazy part is that my note card did not make the trip to Lakeland, the training headquarters for the Detroit Tigers. As a matter of fact, I had pretty much forgotten about it. And to tell you the truth, I don't think it is a coincidence that my career ended at the one place where I forgot to bring my constant reminder of my life's mission. It was almost as though I thought I had made it. Maybe, without the note card on my wall, I forgot that my dream was to play shortstop for the Tigers in the major leagues, not in the minor leagues. After this experience, I have always remembered to write my goals down and keep them visible.

STEP 5: FIND A PARTNER

The next step is one I found major success with as a performance coach, and currently as a real estate agent. I use it with all of my clients, and because of that, it's become a crucial part of the **Hustle 'Til It Happens** program.

Here it is: **Find someone to share your journey with.**

This person will be called your accountability partner. He or she will share your goal, your process, and your progress. You may want to do the same for them.

Choose carefully. Your success will partially depend on it. There should be no power relationship with this person (as in an employee or a boss) — that would make it too complicated. On the other hand, it isn't important if the person already has faith in you and your ability to reach your dream. It's only important that they're engaged and will give you honest feedback when needed.

So make a list of a few people you think would be great accountability partners.

Again, choose wisely. I chose my business partner Jennifer because she is a machine. We check in daily and report to each other what the other has going on, or if we're struggling with something. Having Jennifer on my team has been a blessing. We keep each other focused and moving forward and, in turn, we keep those around us focused and moving forward.

Why It Works

Dominican University performed a study on the success of written goals versus unwritten goals, but then they took it a step further. Dominican University broke participants up into five groups.

Group 1: Unwritten goals

Group 2: Written goals

Group 3: Written goals and action commitment

Group 4: Written goals, action commitment, and sending both to a supportive friend

Group 5: Written goals, action commitment, and sending both to a supportive friend plus sending a weekly progress report to the friend

Participants were allowed to choose their own goals and the goals varied widely. After all the research was done, it was proven that groups 4 and 5 had the highest success rates. Those were the only two groups that had "accountability partners." Group 5 had the highest success rate of all. The study proved that *the simple act of writing down the goal and sharing it with a partner made it more likely to happen.*

Dawson and Brett

Writing a goal down and finding an accountability partner can prove to be life changing, and for two of my coaching clients, it was just that.

I put this concept to work with Dawson and Brett, high school students in Traverse City, Michigan. Both of them are 6'4, right-handed pitchers, and both have similar goals.

For the first six months, we worked on the mental game once a week on a conference call. We also created a process they implemented on their own on a daily basis. (Mental work was much needed because baseball is such a game of failure. If you can't handle it, you won't play very long, and the time you do spend playing will be very difficult.) The outcome was that mentally, both boys were more prepared and both handled success and failure better, but the huge take-away was the fact that *neither one made any sensational gains physically.*

Dawson and Brett's commitment to the mental game came from day one, but I could not get them to stay on the consistent physical workout routine that I'd outlined for them. They saw gains when they did it, but they were inconsistent and, therefore, the result was worthless. I was perplexed, and even frustrated.

As I began to reflect, I realized that our weekly talks were only about the mental side: they would tell me how they used the tools we implemented, how they made them feel, and if they were working. I also realized that I was holding them accountable only *to me*, and that is why the mental work was getting done. But how could I get them to stay accountable on a daily basis in the gym since, at the time, I didn't live in Traverse City and they couldn't afford to hire a personal trainer? I also didn't have the time to go through the mental game *and* the workout on the weekly phone call.

I needed a new plan.

I saw a great opportunity for the two boys to be each other's accountability partner. This is when I called a meeting in Traverse City and implemented the idea. I knew the program was the right program — it had already worked for me and other clients — but this was the first time I used it with distance coaching.

Why did I think they would be great for each other? They played on rival high school teams, yet their summer baseball program brought them together. They were friends and both had a need to improve and compete in order to help their teams win. I brought Dawson and Brett together to formulate a process and tracking method (which we will discuss in the **Create a Process** chapter), and to report to each other and myself on weekly basis.

The plan worked. When we started the practice, both Dawson and Brett improved their physical strength, mental toughness, plus increased their commitment and accountability level. They both began throwing at a higher velocity (much needed), and both lifted more weight than before.

The study from Dominican University supports what I found with Dawson and Brett: writing goals down is well and good, but for great results you need a process and someone to hold you accountable.

STEP 6: BE SPECIFIC

Writing down a specific goal is a vital step in the **Hustle 'Til It Happens** program. The more specific your goal is, the better. A specific goal gives you an exact mission, and we all need an exact mission. All too often people set fuzzy goals, such as, "get better at writing" or "be more positive." These are not goals — they are vague thoughts that inspire little to no action.

Playing in the big leagues was a great dream, but playing shortstop for the Detroit Tigers in the big leagues gave me the specific details to work on and use in my process. Setting this specific goal meant that I had to put intense work into my fielding, as well as my hitting. Had I said, "I want to play left field in the big leagues," my fielding would have been secondary, but as a shortstop, fielding had to be a primary focus of my training.

My coaching experience proved that most people came in with goals that were not only very vague, but also very small.

One goal I often heard was to make the varsity baseball team. The reason this goal is a bad goal is that it's not nearly lofty enough. I coached one young man who aimed for the varsity team, but after some time of digging in and breaking down what he really wanted, it was obvious that his true goal was to play major league baseball for the Chicago Cubs. We did not define his true goal right away — we had a few more stops, such as becoming a starter on varsity or playing at the next level, but once we dug down, we got there.

Another vague goal I heard as a personal trainer was, "I want to lose weight." I would always respond with, "Great, go jump on the treadmill for one hour and you will have successfully achieved your goal." I would then explain why I'd made that comment and we would start the process of setting the proper goal for the right reasons.

"Losing weight" as a goal is vague, and "losing ten pounds" is too small to create serious action unless that ten-pound reduction is your dream weight. What I mostly found when someone said they wanted to lose ten pounds was that the math did not add up.

ME: "What is the number you ultimately want to reach"?

180-POUND CLIENT: "I'd like to get to one-sixty."

Once we admitted that 180 minus 10 does not equal 160, I would then ask them why they aimed so low. Invariably, they said that they were scared to give the real number because they thought I would think they were crazy. (As a side note: the only time I think people are crazy is when they don't believe they can achieve the goals they set.) Once we dug deep, the client would realize the process — of losing weight — would be more successful the **bolder** — or more unrealistic — the goal. This is because massive goals require massive action.

STEP 7: CHECKPOINTS

Vague and small goals can serve a purpose in the goal-setting process — I call them checkpoints, or short-term goals that you need to reach in order to achieve your ultimate goal.

Making the varsity team or losing ten pounds is a checkpoint, and the purpose of checkpoints is to show progress and create confidence through minor successes. I demand that my clients celebrate each checkpoint. The checkpoints will change, the ultimate goal will not.

Checkpoints create momentum, and please do not downplay the importance of momentum in your life. Momentum creates waves of success, faster and faster, because the more good things you do, and the more small successes you achieve, the more you will want to keep enjoying that sense of accomplishment. It is simply amazing.

Be specific in your goal setting.
It will set you up for success and give you an exact purpose.

Harvey Martin

I want to tell you about Harvey Martin, a former player I coached who became a good friend. Harvey played professional baseball with the Milwaukee Brewers organization. When it comes to stating specific goals, Harvey understands the principle perfectly.

Harvey started his college career at Central Michigan University. He had elbow surgery, but about a year later, he hit a serious bump. One day during Harvey's recovery, he was throwing to hitters on the field in what is called a *simulated game*. Suddenly he felt a twinge in his elbow … and he got scared. His mind fired off all kinds of fearful thoughts: Had he put in a year of rehab for nothing? Would his elbow never fully heal? Would he ever get into the big leagues, which was his one big dream?

This is the moment when Harvey and I became linked. He ran into the clubhouse and tried to hide. I followed him because I noticed he was visibly shaken up. I then told Harvey that some other guys were coming inside, and we went out another door so we could talk in private. When Harvey was out the door, I grabbed him and hugged him. Immediately Harvey started to cry, and this is exactly what he needed because it made him more focused than ever before in his life. He realized it was okay to be scared. Not only was it okay, it was *great* because it meant everything he was doing was for a purpose.

The next year, before I ever got to see Harvey pitch in a real game, I took a job at another school. I didn't talk to him for a year, so I didn't know he was very unhappily sitting in the bullpen at Central Michigan. Harvey played the year out, and the following fall I received a phone call out of the blue. As we talked, he shared his thoughts about how he might transfer out of CMU. I listened, then I asked, "Why did you call me?" Harvey then told me something I will never forget. He said, "I know you were only at CMU for a season, and we weren't around each other a lot, but the day you gave me a hug has really stuck with me."

He said it had helped him through the tough time he was facing, and it made him feel comfortable calling me about his current problems. Soon after we talked, I found out that Harvey was transferring to Minnesota State in order to become a starting pitcher instead of pitching from the bullpen. Harvey put up absolutely amazing numbers at Minnesota State, and his hopes of getting drafted were high. He wanted to play pro ball at this point, and he was ready to move forward in his career. In baseball years, Harvey was getting old, so he knew the clock was ticking.

But in a disappointing turn of events, Harvey did not get drafted, and he was upset. In fact he was so upset, he spent the next few weeks feeling sorry for himself. I only make this point because this is not in his character at all. It seemed as though all the hardships he'd faced in his career came crashing down at once.

During this time, Harvey and I talked on a daily basis. I got on the phone with pro scouts to set up workouts for him. Harvey traveled and traveled, but nothing came of the workouts. The thing was, Harvey had one more year of eligibility left at school, and he wanted to turn pro right then. Once the realization set in that he would be back at Minnesota State, Harvey sat down and wrote out a goal for the following season — he was going to be the Division II (DII) Pitcher of the Year. Harvey also shared this goal with everyone. In a way, all of his friends and teammates became his accountability partners.

Great start, but he didn't just write it down, he began to put in the work. And the work he put in led to an undefeated season on the mound. He created a very bold and "unrealistic" goal and then set his sights squarely on performing his daily process. Harvey was the DII Pitcher of the Year the following season.

Exercise:

Send your written goal and your written process to your accountability partner. Provide weekly updates of your progress and why you did not get something done (if that happens) and what you'll do to prevent that happening again in the future. We will discuss tracking progress in the **Create a Process** chapter.

WHAT IS YOUR "WHY"?

Now that you have written down your goal, you need to examine **why** it is your goal. If you do not have a "why," you will not commit to your goal. The "why" keeps you focused and it keeps you hungry.

Find out why the goal is important to you, embrace the "why," and live it.

For me, baseball consumed all my thoughts. When it was soccer or basketball season, I still spent time playing baseball at every opportunity. I loved baseball — playing baseball burned inside of me and honestly, to this day, it is still how some people identify me. People say, "Sam, the baseball guy." There is nothing wrong with being identified by your passion — it simply means that your passion is clear.

There were times when I thought about the money or the fame, but my true motivation was to be the *best*. I wanted to win.

I also love to compete, and I wanted to make a bunch of money so I could help others. To be perfectly honest, one of the main reasons I wanted to make a lot of money was so I could go back to Taylor, Michigan, where I grew up playing ball, and build a top notch Little League facility. I never really thought about huge houses, fast cars, or flying all over the place, but I always wanted to help others. That desire burns greater today than it ever has, and that is my "why."

My "why" is not about competing and winning, rather it's about pursuing my genuine desire to help others. I do love to compete and win, but helping people is the deep-down reason I love doing what I do.

My definition of success is to help others, add value to their life, have fun with what I do, and make money doing it — in that precise order. It was, is, and always will be part of who I am and what I do. I truly enjoy helping people and, more so, helping people live the life they deserve. I've made YouTube videos that anyone can watch for free. I post my own inspirational quotes on Instagram, Twitter, and Facebook. I do these things because *I want to help people live a better life.* I don't get paid to do these things — I do them because they help people get through tough times, and that is what life is all about — for me. I want to return the favor of so many people helping me along my journey. (Okay, that said, I also *do* get paid for helping people. Sometimes more than others, but money isn't the goal for me. My goal is to help people *and* have a ton of freedom.)

STEP 8: IDENTIFY YOUR "WHY"

Be honest about it. It doesn't matter what your "why" is — it only matters that you know what it is and that you can articulate it to others through your actions.

One thing to remember is what Simon Sinek says in his famous TED Talk, "People do not buy what you do; they buy **why** you do it." This is important because people like to be a part of something genuine. If they feel you are a genuine human being who cares about others it will show. They will embrace your **why** and may even help tell your story.

PART II: REFINE YOUR GOALS

WILL YOUR GOALS ALLOW YOU TO BE AUTHENTIC?

Even if you have firmly set a goal, you'll still need to fully evaluate it to make sure it lines up with your value system. I didn't do that at first, and ended up spending four years owning a baseball facility I didn't want and working mega-hours. I'm not trying to tell you that your **chosen** goal is not your **actual** goal, I'm just challenging you to look deeper in order to speed up the process of reaching success. I want you to get there quicker than I did, and that is what this book is all about.

STEP 9: BE YOURSELF

Being authentic means clearly letting the world know who you are and what your true intentions are.

So, ask yourself if your goal will allow you to be authentic — to simply be yourself in all aspects of your life.

Why is this important? Being authentic is important because people (possibly girlfriend/boyfriend, employers, employees, customers) want to surround themselves and support others who share their values and perspectives. If you are authentic, you will never have to worry about someone not liking you because it won't matter. It won't matter *because you will like yourself.*

All you can do is paint the picture you want people to see. Those who are attracted to that picture will hover towards you, just as you will hover towards others who paint a picture that attracts you.

> Being authentic means that you are consistently sending out the same message about yourself. You will never have to worry about doing image repair or about somebody getting the wrong impression of you.

Please understand that "authentic" is what *you* want it to be, not what you think it *should* be. If you want to make a ton of money, say it. If you want to give back and help others, prove it with your actions. Society often places the people with the most altruistic intentions under a very detailed microscope because they want to know if it's real — and what's "real" is only reflected by what you do on a daily basis.

My authentic self is someone who wants to have fun, live on my own terms, and help others. This is the authentic me. Of course I have to make a living — I will never try to hide that. Just like everyone else, I have to pay bills and save for the future, so I'm not ashamed to say I *must* make money. But it's important to note that there is no value above my actual needs that I place on money. For example, I do not have a goal of making a million dollars per year. If that happened, I wouldn't be upset, but that's not what I chase. I chase value, and if I add enough value I get paid. But what I love is that I don't get paid until I add a ton of value.

What Are Values?

> When it comes to your goal and your **why**, understand that your goal must align directly with your values.

And what are values? By definition, they are principles or standards of behavior and judgments of what one finds important in life. By understanding this definition, you can begin to **Hustle 'Til It Happens**, and you can also set goals that align with your values.

Tell the Truth

It often happens that a person will set a goal to, for example, "help people" because they think it will impress others and allow them to make a lot of money.

Therefore their highest priority isn't to help people, it's to make a lot of money. They are only using the idea of helping others in order to impress people and get rich. Instead of just admitting "I want to make $5 million," they hide behind a goal they think will come across as more socially acceptable.

The problem, then, is that even though this person is talented and has the ability to make a lot of money, they are focused on the wrong thing (giving back). Hiding behind one goal to get at another — besides being unauthentic — makes the success of their true goal harder, maybe even impossible. It takes a lot of energy to be unauthentic, too much energy.

Please note that I am in no way saying that giving back is the wrong thing to focus on. I am simply saying that for the person in the example, giving back as a primary goal doesn't authentically line up with their value system and therefore is a lie and a waste of time.

Exercise:

→   Write down your "why" and your values

→   Describe your authentic self

DO A COST-BENEFIT ANALYSIS

A cost-benefit analysis is a "systematic approach to estimating the strengths and weaknesses of alternatives that satisfy transactions, activities or functional requirements for a business." Obviously we are talking about your life, not a specific business, but if you want to start a business, a cost-benefit analysis is vitally important because it will tell you how badly you really want it.

Everything we do in life comes at a cost. If we want to get someplace faster, we fly. But it's more expensive to fly a family of four from Michigan to California than it is to drive. The benefit is the time we save. If time is not an issue, then it's more beneficial to drive and save the money. Other items you would have to consider in this particular cost-benefit analysis is the wear and tear on the car you drive; spending three full days in your car with the family (especially true if you have young kids or teens); the cost of gas, motel and food; and your own ability to sit in a car for three days. In its simplest form, this process is all about determining what you are going to give up in order to get what you want. In high school, I had to do a cost-benefit analysis every single weekend when it came to my social life. Was drinking with my friends worth the possibility of getting caught and losing my chance of playing college baseball and ultimately my dream of playing in the big leagues? The answer was an unmistakable no.

In order to break this example down clearly, I'll show you four examples of how I finally got to my current choice of careers by using a cost-benefit analysis.

COST-BENEFIT ANALYSIS OF PLAYING IN THE BIG LEAGUES

Question: Decide if playing shortstop for the Detroit Tigers is worth the following sacrifices

Cost: Time with friends, time with family, not eating junk food, being sore, giving up my high school social life

Benefit: Living the life I intend to live, having freedom, money, being able to give back

Analysis: I will do whatever it takes because I want this worse than anything in the world

COST-BENEFIT ANALYSIS OF CONTINUING TO OWN
AN INDOOR BASEBALL FACILITY

Question: Decide if it is advantageous to continue operating this business?

Costs: Time, aggravation of dealing with the landlord, aggravation of dealing with angry parents, internal struggle between making people pay for lessons and my belief that lessons are pretty worthless in their current state, the effort and time required to make major changes to the business structure, etc.

Benefits: Be my own boss and potential earnings of $100,000 per year

Analysis: I am out of here

NOTE: I was worn down by this business, so making the needed changes was simply not an option for me. By needed changes, I mean complete overhaul. I simply could go no further because it did not mean enough to me.

In the next example, the choice came down to staying in coaching or moving into a career as a full-time speaker and performance coach. At the time I was coaching at Alma College and my speaking career had already begun.

COST-BENEFIT ANALYSIS OF MOVING INTO A CAREER AS FULL-TIME SUCCESS COACH AND SPEAKER

Goal: Create a performance coach and speaking business

Cost: Giving up my current comfort of a paycheck every two weeks, giving up my post as a college baseball coach, short-term financial loss, working with students, athletes and adults daily, etc.

Benefits: Help people improve their lives, make a difference with many different people, authentically enjoy what I do, gain time freedom, make my own schedule, long-term possibility of financial freedom

Analysis: Although I will miss working with the players on a daily basis, I will still be coaching, and now I will be able to help more kinds of people at once

NOTE: Although I still help people I was never able to truly turn this into a sustainable business model for myself and I realized that I lost a lot of quality time with friends. It was lonely work, and I like to deal with people daily. In the end I realized that a coaching and speaking business was not for me, but something I would like to do on the side

---

COST-BENEFIT ANALYSIS OF A CAREER IN REAL ESTATE

Goal: Become the top producing real estate agent in terms of units sold in Traverse City, investing in multi-family homes in order to create a passive income, and creating the best team in town

Cost: Feeling like I am letting people down by giving up my coaching business. Also, losing the income created through the coaching business, starting over, and possibly spending all the money I'd saved to get my real estate business off the ground

Benefit: Ability to fulfill all three points on my list of helping people, having fun with my job, and making money. Leaving behind a toxic business venture. Helping friends, family, and new clients sell their current home and buy their new home. Creating a business that will allow me to invest in order to help my family have a secure future. Having a chance to still speak and help people with their goals as new agents come into the business. The last one is a huge plus

Analysis: Time to dive right in on this new venture and make this goal a reality with no regard for the possibility of going broke

Before you start thinking all of these changes mean I quit a lot, please understand that other than not making the big leagues, I have reached every goal I have written down.

In life, we sometimes realize that we are chasing the wrong dream. A good friend of mine once told me, "If your most recent decision is robbing you of happiness, simply make a new decision." Consistency and persistence are hugely important, but if you find yourself walking away from something because you realize you're not passionate about it, *you are not quitting. You're actually starting.* You've decided to leave something you dislike to begin your new path towards happiness and fulfillment.

The cost-benefit analysis is a great tool if you're in a job and debating whether to leave — and jump to a new goal immediately— or stay a while to work toward your new decision. Of course, there's always the alternative of simply doing nothing.

STEP 10: MAKE YOUR COST-BENEFIT ANALYSIS

Use the tool of a cost-benefit analysis. I know it can get you going or get you unstuck. It's simply a must-do when it comes to the **Hustle 'Til It Happens** program.

With this exercise, you will save years — years that I certainly misspent making career mistakes. Failing to do a cost-benefit analysis literally cost me thirteen years of chasing the wrong dreams. I learned from these experiences and met great people and, in that sense, they weren't failures. But when I finally did the analysis, I realized I was chasing the wrong goal in order to achieve my dream of helping people, having fun, and freedom. I would ask you right now to stop reading and do a cost-benefit analysis of your goals to refine them further.

PLAN A ONLY

Texting and driving is illegal because it's extremely dangerous. It distracts us from the most important task: driving safely. The same is true with setting a goal and then creating a back-up plan. Although people list multi-tasking as a skill, there is nobody inherently good at multi-tasking because when we multi-task both tasks get deprived of the full attention they need.

When it comes to goal-setting, Plan B is the biggest enemy of Plan A. You should have a Plan A *only*. Having a Plan B allows you to feel secure with failure and makes it easier to quit when things get tough. A back-up plan also takes your focus off of Plan A. Anything that takes your focus away from the ultimate goal is detrimental to success.

When Khalil Greene, a former first-round pick of the MLB draft, was asked by a grade school teacher what he wanted to do when he grew up, he answered, "Play professional baseball." When the teacher told him he needed a back-up plan, he didn't have one. A back-up plan would have been a distraction from his goal.

Plan for Action

I am not suggesting that you drop out of high school, quit your job, or do anything drastic because, quite simply, I don't personally know your situation, so suggesting such a thing would be irresponsible. What I am saying is, create a Plan A, and if you currently have a job that you must stay in to cover your bills, then get up earlier or go to bed later or skip your nightly TV time and glass of wine to make

HUSTLE 'TIL IT HAPPENS

your plan come alive. If it really means something to you, none of this will seem like a huge sacrifice.

On the other hand, if you are single and nobody is counting on you for support, taking the leap of faith might be the right move. But, again, I cannot positively say it is. You must do a budget and assess your situation on an individual basis before making any earth-shattering decisions.

Also, your Plan A may have a lot of components to it, and each one must be met. These are the **checkpoints** that we talked about earlier. For example, making it to the big leagues had a lot of checkpoints before it was going to come true. I knew I was not going to get drafted out of high school, so that meant I had to finish high school, get good enough grades to get into college, and then continue to pass classes in order to stay eligible.

Pivoting (Is It Time Move On?)

Let's say you have your Plan A. You work hard, but you're coming up short over and over again. Let's say you no longer have the resources to continue down this path. Or, maybe you have the resources, but you realize this path no longer suits you.
Now what?

Now is when you make a new Plan A. People may say, *this is quitting*, but its not quitting, it is cutting your losses — or, as I call it, "pivoting."

Whether you are pivoting and/or cutting your losses, the ability to move forward shows maturity and growth.

And no regrets, because you haven't been wasting your time. All along your journey — just like my journey chasing the big league dream — you've picked up a work ethic, a mindset, a competitive spirit, strong relationships, and other tools that transfer into everything you do in life.

So, if you happen to come up short of your ultimate goal (Plan A), you simply regroup and use the tools you have to work on the next step of your life.

For me, once my professional career ended, I used my credibility along with my ability to connect with and help people to open up an indoor baseball facility. Although my career as a shortstop was over, my dream of being successful and helping others was still intact. During my big league journey, I'd picked up habits that transcended sports and was able to fall back on those habits and skills to start my business, just like you will be able to do if your Plan A fails.

I talk about failure because it is real. Failure should not be scary, and it should not make you shy away from taking the plunge. If anything, it should give you a heightened awareness of the situation and pull out the competitor in you. Failure should fuel your work ethic, it should drive you and make you more organized and prepared. Remember, failure will always be there — sitting, watching, and waiting for you to quit. But I urge you to keep pushing until you exhaust all your options and, at that point, you will have no shame in changing directions. Even exhausted, you can still stand up, dust yourself off, regroup, and get right back to grinding on your next Plan A. We will talk more about how to face and handle the thought of failure in the **Accept Failure** chapter.

Those Nagging Thoughts

In 2009, the idea of being a collegiate baseball coach started to enter my mind. When this happened, I kept telling myself, *What are you thinking? You own a baseball facility. Stay the course!* But the thought kept nagging at me. As I explained earlier, when a thought keeps nagging at me, I must listen and see if there is any validity to it.

I began to take inventory of my life and realized that the baseball facility was failing to provide what I needed. The facility was only fulfilling two of my three pillars for true happiness, so I quickly decided it was time to make a new Plan A.

Next, I did what I always do: I wrote down my goal, then started to work on a process of attainment. I wanted to start at the Division I level — which is pretty bold — but that's what I wanted. I began talking to people, sending emails, making phone calls. Finally, a position at Central Michigan University came open. I went through an extensive interview process … and got the job. Chalk another one up for written goals!

But once the goal was attained, I found a problem. My perception of what a college coach did, and the actual reality of what a college coach does, was way off.

Being a college coach is as much an office job as it is coaching. There is a ton of paperwork, emails, phone calls, meetings, scheduling, event planning, and more. Nonetheless, I stuck with it, mainly because I'm a baseball guy and that is what I thought I had to do with my life — baseball things. I spent four years trying to fit a square peg into a round hole. The one great thing that came from being a baseball coach was the free time during the holidays due to the school schedule. But, I was only fulfilling one of the three pillars of happiness, and that is completely unacceptable.

My failed Plan A led to a new Plan A. During Christmas break in the winter of 2012, I spoke for the first time in front of an audience. It was thrilling, and I started to research speakers — what they did, and how they did it. I began to fall in love with the idea. This was my Plan A of the future.

At this point in life, things had changed and I could not just quit coaching, so I started a side-hustle in order to fulfill my other pillars of happiness. I spent three years toying with the idea, honing my skills, working hard, watching speakers, and researching content. At the end of it, I formulated a plan and dove in headfirst.

On January 6, 2014, I left the world of college baseball and started a full-time performance coaching and speaking business. At this point, I was so sure of this plan that I walked away from college baseball with only one gig lined up for $1,500. But I quickly found the freedom I had been looking for, and my business took off. Everything began to line up, and before I knew it, I had started a lucrative business that allowed me the freedom I had always wanted. Chalk another one up to written goals!

There's a fine line between "giving up" and "regrouping."
If you find that your Plan A —

a) doesn't meet your values, or

b) it just wasn't meant to be despite your most intense efforts.

— you have one option: make a new "Plan A" and chase it with the same undying fury you had for your original "Plan A."

More About Pivoting

In the summer of 2015, my performance coaching/baseball business had its most successful season to date. By "most successful," I mean that we had the most number of teams in our program's history, we put more kids into college than any other year, and my partner and I had made the most money from the business yet. To most people, this sounds like success. The only problem was, we also had more complaints that year than ever before, and there was a hint of division in the group. It seemed like the more money we made, the more parents were upset with us. Also, the more kids we helped get into college, the more the parents whose kids didn't get into college would complain.

I was at a crossroads. The money I was making was only just enough to live off of, and the headaches were getting bigger and bigger.

The question was, should I dig in harder or let go and pursue something more fulfilling? Was this the sign I needed to show me that baseball had pretty much run its course in my life? I had given all I could to the kids I'd coached, but I hadn't been able to better my own life.

One day, I was at the gym and talking to my partner about a phone call from a disgruntled parent. It seemed we were both at the end of our ropes. While we were standing at the counter talking, I actually made the statement, "If I receive one more call from a parent complaining about how bad we're doing, I will be a real estate agent within the next month." My partner laughed, and I left the gym. I got in my car and made it a quarter of a mile down the road before my phone rang. "Hey there," I said, because I saw the parent's name pop up. What ensued was an ass-chewing regarding playing time and exposure for their kid. The conversation ended, and instead of going home, I made a left. I went to the office of Chuck Geer at Coldwell Banker.

Failing My Way to Success

True enough, I had already been exploring new Plan A options. At the gym, I got to know a few agents who seemed to actually like their jobs and were able to do more than just get by. Chuck was a friend from the gym and a seasoned real estate agent. He gladly talked me through the process and set up an interview with a broker. I discussed my ambitions with the broker and, before I left the office, I signed up for my class. That was Wednesday, August 29, 2015. I took the class the very next week, and then took and passed the state test on September 9, 2015. After the test, I drove to my office and started working.

Like always, I jumped into real estate with goals, and like always, they were huge and **bold**. I was very clear on the "why" of pursuing real estate: I wanted to start a team and I wanted to own multi-family investment properties in order to set my family up for a successful future. It's in my blood to work as part of a team — it brings out the best in me and, I think, I am able to bring out the best in others in turn. Most agents do not start a career in real estate like this, but I knew what I wanted. I even set my email up as sam@flamontgroup. com because I knew where I was going. People often laughed when I told them my email. "Group? Didn't you just start?" I never paid attention to it. I just got back to work.

Before starting as a real estate agent, I'd been kicking the idea around and watching training videos on YouTube. Like always, I wanted to be prepared and I wanted to have a process to follow in order to reach my goals. Watching the videos, I quickly learned that real estate was going to be a challenge — it was going to sometimes be uncomfortable, and there was going to be a good chance of failure — or, at least, the chance that I'd completely run out of money before I had enough closings to stay afloat.

All of this made me excited, it made me want to compete, and so my next move was very important: I calculated how much time I had before I ran out of money. I realized I only had about six months. The problem with six months is that everyone I talked to said it takes six to eight months before a new agent makes any money. Again, the feeling of excitement ran through my body because I love the feeling of pressure. I have always felt that my game rises to the next level when I'm under pressure.

So, when I got back to my office after passing the text, I sat down at my computer, pulled out my pad of paper that had a huge list of "for sale by owners," and I began calling them. Once I made it through the list, I hit the streets and started knocking on doors. I introduced myself to hundreds of people in my first week.

I also began talking to all the top-producing agents because I wanted to know what they were doing — but I also really wanted to know what they were *not doing*. Why? Because I needed to find a playing field that I could create and dominate. It wasn't that I was scared of competing, it was simply that I wasn't yet prepared to compete with the top agents. I needed to create a playing field in which they didn't exist.

I took some agents to lunch, I sat in some of their offices, I always asked questions, and I listened. What I heard was that all of the top agents were doing the *same thing*, which is probably why they were top agents in the first place. But they'd been in the game for ten-plus years, some thirty-plus years. I didn't have their experience, but I was armed with something more powerful than experience — I had questions, I listened, and I had a willingness to put myself in uncomfortable situations, such as cold calling and door knocking. I knew that at some point in the future I would be using the advice they were giving me, but I also knew that at the present time, I needed to do all the things they were not. My idea was to fail, fail a lot, and fail fast. The more I failed, and the quicker I failed, the sooner I would become successful. So what did I do? I chose actions like cold calling and door knocking in order to get uncomfortable and *fail my way to success.*

And here I am — after years of chasing the wrong dream, of being foolish enough to believe I deserved everything I wanted and crazy enough to think I could have it, I created the best Plan A of all time. My reason for going into real estate was that it gave me freedom to control my schedule, a chance to help people, and a chance to make money and no longer stress about money. My new Plan A was to dive in headfirst and not look back.

CREATE A PROCESS, FOCUS ON YOUR DAILY GOALS

Some people will tell you to be process-oriented, while others will tell you that you should focus on the results — one thing I know for a fact: these two concepts are married.

Anyway, the argument isn't so much which is better. To put it simply, the results you want will help you create your daily process, and your daily process will lead you to the results you want.

To be honest, it is a chicken and egg argument to me.

My buddy Ty Rogers was a baseball coach at Indiana and now works for Jim Harbaugh at the University of Michigan He believes a process is necessary, but he chooses to focus his attention on the end result. Jeff Opalewski, associate head coach and recruiting coordinator for Central Michigan University, says the opposite: "I consider myself process-oriented, and I definitely am when it comes to most of my strengths, although I also have some result-oriented tendencies." So, the focus varies from person to person, but one fact remains: you must have a process or you will wander aimlessly.

Personally, I will say this: my goals came to me quicker when I focused my mind less on the end result and more on the daily process. When I focused on the results I wanted, I just kept seeing how far I had to go. As soon as I switched my focus to the daily process, I begin to see how far I've come.

Process is by far the most important part of the **Hustle 'Til It Happens** program because, if you're going to reach for extremely difficult goals, you will need a constant reminder of how far you have come.

As Tony Robbins explains, "certainty" is an essential human need, and your process will create certainty. He also says we all need "uncertainty" because it makes us feel alive.

It's an absolute guarantee that we will all face some sort of uncertainty in our lives, and we'll surely experience it on our quest to live our dreams. But when this happens, it will be your **process** that will give you the tools to handle the uncertainty and adversity.

STEP 11: FIND THE STEPS, CREATE A PROCESS

Research the basic actions it will take for you to reach your goal. For example, on my quest to play professional baseball, I had to lift, run, hit, field, stretch, and eat healthy food. Once I knew these things, I set out to create my daily process.

Exercise:

1: Research what other people in your chosen field have done to get where they are.

Once you collect your research, you may want to personalize actions to your particular goals. But remember to strongly consider the experience and wisdom of those who have gone before you. If your research shows commonalities, it's a safe assumption that those are necessary steps. Make a list.

Example: To start a real estate career, I need to

> learn to make calls, write letters, schedule appointments, talk with other agents, go to trainings, negotiate contracts, manage emotions, etc.

2: Write out the process.

It sounds crazy, but this where most people quit. They find out how much work their dream is going to take and, instead of committing to do what it takes to live their dream life, they settle for average — they find a job that will give them a paycheck for doing just enough to not get fired. This step is where you separate yourself from most people.

Note: A process is different from a list. The process is something we do every single day, or as many days as we lay out for ourselves. A list is a group of projects that vary from day to day. Part of my process now as a real estate agent is to complete my daily list.

Example: to learn to make calls — sit in with experienced agents

research strategies on-line

start a file to record successes / failures

Also, as discussed in the **What is Your "Why"?** chapter of the book, you need to write down your **checkpoints,** or short-term goals. As a performance coach, I had my clients divide a sheet of paper with a line down the middle. On one side, they wrote their process. On the other side they wrote their next checkpoint. Their ultimate goal is already written on a note card and will not change.

3: Create a point system and grade yourself.

As you write down your process, include the number of times you need to do each item. In this way, you are creating a point system, and the point system will give you a grade each week, a grade that will reflect your discipline and determination.

If you are currently in a job and know you'll have to pursue your dream part-time, make sure you write down your process accordingly. Below is a very basic and abbreviated example of the daily process I assigned myself in my pursuit to play professional baseball. Note that I included all seven days in the week because this was my full-time job. You can and should adjust accordingly.

BASEBALL PROCESS:

Hit seven days per week

Lift five days per week

Visualize five minutes per day

Do breathing exercises daily

Write in a positivity journal seven days per week

Run 60 yard sprints M-W-F

Practice ground balls seven days per week

In the above example, I gave myself one point for every task. Therefore, hitting seven days a week equaled seven points, with forty-one points possible. I put a check mark next to the step after I finished each one. If I only hit six times a week, instead of seven, but I met my goal with all the others, I would give myself a score of 40/41, or 97 percent. It should go without saying that 100 percent is the desired score.

It is important to write down why you missed a day or why you missed a particular activity because it will allow you to reflect on what is going on. If you missed hitting on Monday, write down why. Were you hurt? Or did you just decide it was not important and wanted a day off for no good reason? Did you not feel like getting up at 5 a.m. to work on your dream business before you went to work, or were you up all night taking care of a sick child? Being completely honest with yourself is the most important part of this because it will show you the true reason you missed a day. Maybe your car broke down and you simply could not get to the hitting facility. That is valid. Then, ask yourself, is there another option for you to get the work done without going to the indoor facility? If not, okay. But if there's another option, that's not okay. What I mean by this is, if you live in Michigan and it is January, there is a good chance you can't hit outside, and maybe you don't have a garage to put a tee in. You can see that this is valid, but anything short of doing what is needed or actually available is not valid.

To show you how this program works for more than athletics, I'll give you an example of what I did when I became the sales manager at a health club. I was brought into the club for one reason only, and that was to increase memberships in order to increase revenue. Once I proved I could solve that problem, I was given other tasks to solve as well.

The first thing I did was look at the current sales system. I quickly found out that there was *no* system. There were no dedicated sales people and no specific sales training for the staff. Whoever was standing at the front desk was responsible for conducting the membership sale when a prospect called or came through the door. No wonder membership numbers had become so stagnant!

I went to work on creating a system for every nuance of the sales process. I wanted to know how many prospective members came in, and I also wanted to quantify the percentage of time we closed the sale on the spot. The first thing I did was create a visitor log-in system and trained staff how to use it. We rehearsed how to conduct a tour or handle a phone inquiry with a specific script. We even went over greetings for prospects and discussed how to retain existing gym members. The last thing I did was raise membership rates so that we could offer people what they actually wanted. People thought I was crazy to raise a gym membership by $100 per year, but it lined up with the image the club was trying to create — that of a high-end club that offered great value and was safe and clean. Memberships skyrocketed and people were happy to pay the new fee because they received what they wanted. We offered free group classes with a year contract, which meant I had to know how many new memberships would be required to cover the cost of the class instructors for one year. I found that out quickly, and we achieved it in the first three weeks of the new membership drive. Below is an example of my daily sales process. I was also a manager at the gym, so I had other duties, but this is an abbreviated system of what I did daily in order to make sure the club was growing and improving.

SALES PROCESS:

Check the prospective member log-in box M–F

Check the new memberships in the new membership box M–F

Quantify the percentage of sales that were completed M–F

Identify why the percentage went up (or down) from week to week F

Talk with desk staff about their confidence and knowledge level of the new system M–F

Train people on the system and how to use the script so that no matter who handled the sale it was handled the same way M–F

Look for new ways to increase revenue or decrease expenses M–F

> The items on your process are tasks you deem **extremely important** to the long-term success of your dream or goal.

A process not only lowers my anxiety, it also keeps me on track and allows me to schedule meetings, lunches, phone calls, etc., because I know how much time I have and when I will have the time. As a note, I also explicitly schedule fun activities, so that I can create a balance in my life.

Just like in the baseball example, my sales process had a point system. At the end of the week, you should total everything up and file that week's process sheet either in a paper or computer file. You then create the next one. The purpose of saving these sheets is to show yourself how far you have come and how much work you have put in to get closer to your dream.

4: Now, get out a calendar and start scheduling the steps you will follow day by day.

These are your daily goals. As you accomplish them, you will get one step closer to your dream.

5: Find an accountability partner and text or email your results weekly.

We have already discussed this so I will not beat it to death, but make sure you take this step very seriously.

By writing down your process, making check marks, adding up your score, sending them to your accountability partner, and then filing them away, you are seeing your daily successes and gaining confidence. Also, when things get tough and the adversity begins to feel like too much, you can look back on all of these sheets and say, "Wow, look at everything I have done to get this far. I just have to keep pushing and hustling."

This is where your accountability partner can help you. Your partner should encourage you with the successes you've had and how far you've already come. Although I believe that some people need a swift kick in the behind once in a while, I'm also a firm believer that kind words and actions from a friend, a family member, or a coach get better results.

Everything we do in the **Hustle 'Til It Happens** program is to help create confidence, because when things get hard, it is imperative that you continue to proceed with certainty.

Remember, at the end of the process is the result, and the desired result is daily improvement, which is why we break it down to a daily process. If we improve everyday, it will keep us going and allow us to relentlessly and fearlessly pursue our dream.

ACCEPT FAILURE AS AN OPTION AND PROCEED WITH CERTAINTY

Accepting the possibility of failure is the hardest part of the **Hustle 'Til It Happens** program because most people have a severe fear of failure or embarrassment. This is the first step where I am asking you to actually take action on your dreams. Every other step so far has been about getting prepared to take action.

You've heard the saying, "Failure is not an option." Although it's a great thought, in order to truly chase your dreams, you must embrace the prospect of failure. Not only must you embrace it, you must run directly *toward* failure if you want to be successful.

The road to success and the road to failure is actually the same road, and it runs in exactly the same direction. Therefore, if you run from failure you are actually running from success.

I live my life by the notion that when you allow failure to become an option, you allow greatness and success to also become an option. Running toward failure means you are taking steps to pursue your dream.

In the **Hustle 'Til It Happens** program, you must love the thought that failure is an option. If you can embrace that concept, you will then find your competitive spirit.

In a conversation with Jake Boss, Michigan State University's head baseball coach, he defined success as "Knowing that you gave your very best effort, regardless of the outcome." If you can use this approach, running toward failure will be a lot less scary.

Failure *can* scare you into inaction, but my hope is that the idea of failure *catapults* you into taking massive action in order to decrease the chances of failure and increase the chances of winning the competition. So far, we have not taken the first actual step. So far, we have been planning our steps and laying them out in order to get prepared and organized for our forthcoming competition with failure. Now we are working hard to embrace the idea that we're letting the possibility of failure and defeat enter our world. We realize that if we don't accept that very real possibility, we are setting up a roadblock and keeping our dreams at a distance.

Regarding failure and its role in the pursuit of success, Jeff Opalewski says, "It's a real part of the process. It typically provides the necessary feedback to allow me to adjust the process to move more directly towards greatness. In that regard, I suppose it is tremendously important."

> Accepting failure as an option is the last step before we launch into massive action. You simply cannot move forward until you accept this reality, because if you move forward with a fear of failure, you are guaranteed to meet your fear quickly.

A lot of people take every single step before this one, but instead of actually thinking about and embracing failure, they choose to ignore it. Ignoring failure before we launch into action only makes it easier to quit at the first sign of adversity. Accepting failure as an option is a process of facing adversity before it hits.

A great example of this is when I started my real estate career by cold calling people who were selling their homes on their own. I knew they really didn't want to talk to me, but I needed to talk to them. It was scary, but once I made the first call and was told "no thank you," I quickly realized I was fine. People weren't cursing me out, they simply didn't want my help. That's okay, but I still ended up listing four houses in my first month from cold calling. Had I not embraced the failure and fear of cold calling, I would have never had that early success which in turn created momentum that has never slowed.

Adversity is an opportunity to quit and fail or persist and be great. If you build adversity into your mental game plan, you will be prepared when it comes. Not only will you be prepared, you will also be less anxious along your journey because you will not be nervous and scared of the unknown. Rather, you will know that adversity lies in front of you.

STEP 12: EMBRACE THE UNKNOWN

The idea of embracing failure is embracing the unknown, and when we embrace these two challenges we quickly begin to accept them. Once we accept them, we can then, and only then, move toward action because our fear will disappear. As our fear fades, it is a sign we are ready to go.

One More Word on Fear

There's a big difference between fear and butterflies in your stomach. Butterflies are a sign that you are alive, fear is a sign that you are not ready to compete.

It is natural to get nervous before a competition, and it actually helps us. Being nervous gives us a heightened sense of awareness. I used to get butterflies before every game I played, even as a pro. Now I get butterflies before I pick up the phone to follow up with someone, or as I am approaching a listing appointment. But it's all good because it means that what I'm doing matters to me. These butterflies signal that I need to use my visualization and breathing techniques (I talk in greater detail on both later) in order to slow my heart rate, bring me back to the moment, and get me prepared to compete.

Fear, on the other hand is paralyzing. Fear keeps us from taking action, and that is why we simply must embrace the fact that **FAILURE IS AN OPTION** when it comes to pursuing our dreams. Once we embrace this fact, we are ready to move onto the next step of proceeding with certainty.

They say the first step is the hardest, and a journey of 1,000 miles starts with the first step, but I disagree. I think the journey of 1,000 miles starts in your mind long before you take the first step. You have to get prepared so that when you take that first step, you are doing so with the utmost confidence that you have the tools to deal with the adversity and that you are heading to something greater. The first step then becomes the easiest because it represents only one of the many steps you're willing to take toward freedom in your life. This is a different perception than most people, but it has served me well throughout my life. It's also worked really well for the people I have coached.

Looking at the Competition

At this point, you have a goal and process in place — it's time to take the first step with confidence. You're confident that you've put in the work and that you're going in the right direction: it's time to step out and compete. Think about it this way: everyone is a competitor, knowingly or not, and even willingly or not.

We all compete, and we are all much more competitive than we give ourselves credit for. Some people may hide behind the mask of "I'm not competitive" in order to protect themselves from feeling hurt or disappointed when they fail or lose. The problem with this is, like it or not, they really *are* competing, and when they look in the mirror, they're not being true to themselves.

Show me someone who is extremely successful in this life and I will show you a fierce competitor. Why am I talking about competing? Because part of proceeding with certainty is *consciously understanding that your goal or dream will require you to compete,* and probably more than just a few times. You not only have to understand the importance of competition, but fully embrace it. This is a key component to the **Hustle 'Til It Happens** program.

For most of us, competition — outside of the world of athletics and games — won't be confrontational in nature. Most competitions are contests of will and being prepared and well organized. For example, if you want to get a bank loan to start a new business, you will need to be extremely prepared and organized in order for the bank to give you the money. In this competition, you can't be confrontational or physical — that would clearly be detrimental to your chances of receiving a loan, and possibly cost you your freedom.

FORMS OF COMPETITION THAT ARE OFTEN OVERLOOKED:

→ Class Rank
→ ACT/SAT Scores
→ Job Interviews
→ College Entrance Interviews
→ Job Promotions
→ Pick-up games
→ Sales
→ People buying your product over someone else's

Anytime you have to persuade somebody to give you something — a gig, money, or a job — you are in a competition. You're not only competing with other applicants you don't know, you're competing for the attention and approval of the person you're trying to get to give you what you want.

It's important to remember that most of the steps needed for you to compete — and win — have already been completed at this point in time. You've researched, created your process, made your checkpoints — *you are prepared.* And now it's time to put the preparation in motion and go get your dreams. The more specific you are with your goals and your process, the more confident, comfortable, and prepared you will be.

STEP 13: MAKE THEM JUDGE YOU

When it comes to proceeding with certainty, one thing I always say is, **Make Them Judge You**. You see, people are going to judge you regardless of whether or not you reach for a big goal. So my thought is, put yourself out there and **Make Them Judge You** for what you really want to do.

As someone who is extremely driven, I am usually judged for working too much, not spending enough time with friends, never turning my phone off, or any other number of reasons. The truth is, I truly feel that I am *always* working and I am *never* working. What does that mean? It means that I take great pleasure in my work and don't feel the need to escape from it.

> Anytime anyone is being judged for the things they are trying to accomplish in life, that's a good thing. It means they're actually doing something worth talking about.

So stop worrying about what others think about you. In fact, give them something to talk about! This is your life and your dream. Don't give others the power to keep you from it. Give yourself the power to be judged by others who are too scared to go after their own **bold** and "unrealistic" dream.

The understanding that failure is an option and is not fatal or final will help you with this step. A failed attempt does not make you a failure, but it will make you stronger and more determined, especially if you have a strong desire to compete and be successful. Remember, I failed trying to reach my goal of making it to the big leagues, but my understanding of failure and the fact that I was driven to be successful allowed me to regroup and:

→ Make a New Plan A

→ Accept Where I Was

→ Create a Process

→ Proceed with Certainty

In my journey to my new Plan A, you would have never known that I spent the last ten years of my life working toward a goal that I failed to reach.

One of my favorite quotes of all time is three words in length and comes from Steve Jobs in response to a critic of the IPod. He said, "Real artists ship." What that means is, everyone has ideas, but a true artist moves boldly to take an idea from concept to reality. A real artist isn't afraid to let the world judge them. They set their plan free, for better and, sometimes, for worse. It may be a smash hit or a miserable failure, but real artists never achieve their dreams unless they set their ship free. Remember your first iPhone? I bet you now own an entirely different model. Why? Because *real artists ship*. So may you set your ship free with courage and conviction. I can promise you this: *you will never wonder what might have been*.

BE CONSISTENT, PERSISTENT, AND PATIENT: THREE KEY FACTORS OF SUCCESS

STEP 14: BE CONSISTENT

When it comes to any goal, the ability to be consistent will keep you headed in the right direction. Your process gives you direction, so you might think being consistent should be easy ... but it isn't always.

Since the **Hustle 'Til It Happens** program relies heavily on process, it's no coincidence that being consistent is extremely important. To put it simply, it's hard to have consistent actions without a process. If your actions are not consistent, what you have is randomness and you will not succeed.

No doubt about it, we are very easily distracted. In fact, the average person changes his or her focus every ten seconds, and it's only getting worse with the relentless distraction of technology and social media platforms. How many times have you sat down to type an email, then seen a news flash on your web browser that you simply had to read? Every minute it feels like something else grabs your attention. Not only are you distracted, but the distraction makes you lose your place, which means you have to find it again. Being consistent is an extremely difficult task, if for no other reason than sometimes *life happens.*

A common theme throughout this book has been confidence and the ability to create confidence. One thing that creates confidence is certainty, and one thing that creates certainty is consistency. Therefore, **being consistent creates confidence.**

Create Consistency by Watching Your Daily Results Improve Through Your Actions

I love to lift weights, and I love to lift heavy weights, so I reached out to Josh Ledford for help. Josh is a guy I once coached, and later we became friends. Josh is excellent at lifting heavy weights, so I asked him to give me a routine in order to improve my strength. Without going into the entire routine, I can tell you that I improved my max squat from 315 pounds to 455 pounds in less than three months. How did I do this? I took the process Josh gave me and I applied *consistent action.* I did not have a goal or a number to reach, I just wanted to lift the heaviest weight I possibly could — and that is what Josh's program allowed me to do … but *only* if I was consistent. My squat went from 315 to 375 pounds very quickly, but then the progress slowed. This is where most people begin to get lost and quit. Our expectation of rapid gains — be it weight loss, weight gain, strength gain, more free time, a better job, or wealth accumulation — kills our consistency because the gains eventually slow down and we feel like we're moving backwards. But, although my squat was only going up ten pounds per week, and eventually five pounds, *it was still going up.*

Failure to see improvement will kill consistency unless we make our check marks and track our progress.

I had the workout Josh gave me — that was my process. But I also kept a journal to show what my max was the previous week and what I could lift now. I might have felt like I wasn't improving, but *I could actually see my results.*

Emotional Control

When it comes to being consistent, our actions are only one part of the story. Some people get really excited when something good happens, and then get really down five minutes later when a negative action occurs. These swings make it very hard to keep our actions consistent because we spend more time celebrating or feeling bad than we do actually moving forward in life.

Emotional consistency takes practice, and the easiest way to stay emotionally consistent is to not let failure or success change your mood too much in either direction. To get your emotions under control, try the visualization exercises in the **SEE IT AND BECOME IT** chapter. Again, this takes practice, but it can be done and needs to be done to give you a greater chance of being successful.

Regardless of whether it is weight lifting, weight loss, or business growth, progress is progress. Nobody wants to work hard and get no results. This is why we need to track our actions, because our actions **are progress** and we must believe that by performing these actions, we are, in fact, improving.

STEP 15: BE PERSISTENT

There are a lot of people who can set a goal, create a process, and even be consistent in their daily actions, but persistence is what separates those that ultimately make it from the ones that quit.

I often tell people that the further they go, the less competition they will face. Why? The further you go, the more people will drop out along the way. And the further you get, the more adversity there is, making even more people quit. Most people can get through one bout of adversity, and a lot can get through a few more quarrels with it, but as they get closer and closer to success or greatness they are simply unable to endure adversity any longer. They get beaten up by setbacks and difficult times and, therefore, decide it will simply be best to exit the highway to success and settle for a life they never intended or wanted — a life they may not even like.

It won't be long before these people begin to feel regret. They'll realize that their new path is actually easier than their old path, but the lack of fulfillment eats at their soul, and this is what I consider *living an average life.*

> When adversity hits, you must realize it is just part of the journey. Once you are able to accept adversity as part of your journey, it will be much easier to understand that what you want out of life **is happening**.

My journey to make the big leagues was full of setbacks, but each time I overcame one, my belief level grew even stronger. My first major setback came at age five when my own father cut me from an all-star team. How could I possibly be the best player on earth when my *own father* did not think I was worthy of an all-star team? At this time, I was not dreaming of the big leagues, but I was by the age of ten. At that age, I was playing shortstop for my Little League team, but when the traveling all-star team was picked, I was moved to the outfield. This may seem silly, but when you are ten and your goal is to be the greatest player ever, this feels like a major setback. My next real setback came in ninth grade when I again lost my starting shortstop job and was moved to right field. Here I was, telling people I was going to the big leagues, but I'd just been moved to right field — right field is where big league dreams go to die when you're that young.

Yes, it upset me, but it never stopped me, and I can honestly look back and say that I was able to keep going because of what I told myself: that people just were not able to see my greatness **YET**, but one day they would. And when they did, *great things would happen.*

Unwavering confidence in who you are and what you are doing is the key to success because it will allow you to understand the principal of **YET**. The principal of **YET** is all about understanding that your goal and dream is going to happen if you keep moving forward — it just hasn't happened **YET**. This principal goes along with the understanding that your goal is actually happening right now, because you are moving toward it.

In the baseball setback story, I also firmly understood that by making three errors in two games back-to-back, plus two errors in a separate game was the real reason I was moved to right field. In ninth grade, I did not lead my team in hitting — or actually in any category — except the category of the guy with a big league dream.

In the summer before tenth grade, I got a weight set from my uncle and put it in my bedroom. This changed my life. Now, not only could I dream of playing in the big leagues and working hard on the field, I could work hard all year and do it on my own time. This is truly when I think my dream became a possibility. Once I saw the changes I was making in my body, there was no stopping me.

But yes, there were more setbacks. Lots of them. Going into my senior year, I was not being recruited by anyone, and that trend continued into the fall, winter, and even the spring. By that point, I had sacrificed time with friends, family, video games, and snow boarding. I'd basically given myself up to my dream. If something didn't help me reach the big leagues, I was not going to make it.

As baseball season approached, the only recruiting call I received was to play Division III football at Hope College. Note that I was awful at football — I was quarterback for a 0–9 team that season. I hated to tackle, yet Hope was recruiting me to pay defensive back! The thought of this made me insane and drove me to work harder in the weight room. I tried to find more time to throw and hit, which was next to impossible at this point in snowy Traverse City, Michigan. Imagine spending the last four years of your life working towards one goal, and when the time came to reap the rewards, there were no rewards to reap. This is what happened to me. As the high school baseball season started, I still did not have a college to play for, which usually means you are not going to play in college.

Then a huge break came my way. My assistant coach called his former coach at Grand Rapids Community College, and he came to see me play at Wyoming Park — the first time a college coach came to see me play. This was a tough day for me, but it was a great day as well. I had a few hits, but I also ruined a perfect game. A perfect game is when the opposing team does not have a single runner reach base. This was the case for Aaron Mendenhall. In the seventh inning with one out, a ground ball came my way. I scooped it up and threw to first base, where the sure-handed Mark Crawford was waiting. But the ball took off on me and tailed up the first base line. I was devastated. I knew I had just ruined Aaron's perfect game. But there was still game left to play. I collected myself and the next pitch Aaron threw turned into another ground ball in my direction. This time, I scooped it up, stepped on second, and threw to first for the game ending double play. Aaron lost the perfect game, but he ended up with a no hitter and faced the minimum number of hitters in a game. I ended up showing the coaches that I was able to bounce back from a mistake and keep moving forward. That, mixed in with a few line drives, earned me an offer to attend Grand Rapids Community College.

However, when the fall season came around at Grand Rapids Community College, it was quickly apparent that I was the low man on the depth chart. This drove me to do what I always did — work so hard that people couldn't ignore me. I quickly began to control the things I could control and people noticed. I won every race we ran in practice, whether it was long distance or a sprint. I fell in love with the leg press machine and quickly showed the team my domination in the strength department as I was maxing out the plates. I'd even ask buddies to sit on it in order to get the weight I needed. When everyone else went home, I ran sprints and did agility work on my own. I didn't do this to impress the coach because, at this point, he was gone. I did it because I had to in order to be a starter and major contributor on the team.

One day we ran sprints in small groups and took a winner from each heat. Then we lined up to see who was the fastest on the entire team. I ended up winning this competition by a decent margin, and although the guys I beat tried to say they didn't care, the coaches clearly did. I hadn't arrived on the team as the fastest player, but the coaches realized that I'd been working harder than anyone. Although this made an impression, I still began the season on the bench and saw only limited action when we headed down south for a few games and split squads. When we came back north, we played Indiana Tech and that's when the starting third baseman got hurt. I felt bad for him, but it gave me the break I needed. Ten games into the season and I finally had the chance to start! That day I went 5–7 with a home run and two doubles and made two great plays in the field. That's how I became the starting third baseman and ended the season leading the team in hitting, plus tying for the lead in home runs.

My work ethic separated me from my teammates and, quite honestly, it did not make me the most popular guy on the team. I didn't hang out and party with the team, and some of the guys didn't like how I always went at things so hard. Maybe they thought it made them look bad, or maybe it made them work harder than they wanted to. Maybe they thought I was too competitive. Whatever the reason, I found out how much they didn't like me when our team took a spring trip. I was the first person to load my bag into the team U-Haul and some kid actually took it off and threw it on the ground before we left Grand Rapids. I only figured it out when we got to the hotel. At that exact moment, *I realized I was doing something right*. I did not go to school to win a popularity contest, and I honestly didn't care if they liked me or not. I was there to continue my mission and help a team win.

This incident only made me more determined to work harder *and* push my teammates even further. I wanted them to be uncomfortable and, at this point, I wanted them to know that I was the one making them uncomfortable. The more people told me to slow down during practice, the faster I ran.

> The thing about being unrealistic with a big dream and bigger work ethic is that you'll often be around people who don't have the same aspirations. When this happens, they'll complain and try to bring you back down to their level. When that fails, they may try to bully you, and when that fails, they will simply leave you alone because they know they can't stop you. The key is to keep hustling, keep grinding, and endure the times when you feel like an outcast. Soon the naysayers will drop out of the competition and you'll be left to do the work you aspire to.

The next fall, I was recruited by Division I schools and officially signed with Western Michigan University in November of 2000. When I arrived at Western Michigan University, the scene quickly became familiar — I was on the bench again. My positions of back-up third baseman, fourth outfielder (which means you're on the bench), and the third-string first baseman, usually means your career is over. It was kind of like being demoted from shortstop to right field in the ninth grade. There was only one thing I knew to do — work so hard that they couldn't ignore me.

And that's what I did. I hit extra, ran extra, lifted more, and simply did everything I could to separate myself from everyone else. Again, the coaches noticed my effort, but that didn't stop them from sitting me in game one. This burned inside of me and my focus grew stronger than ever. In my first at-bat the next day, I got a hit. I added another hit later in the game. Then, the next day, something familiar happened — my friend and starting center fielder went down with an ankle injury. I stepped into center field and played the position in unbelievable fashion. I also got hit after hit. When the center fielder came back, I was moved to left field, but stayed in the starting line-up and in the three hole, which is where coaches generally put their best hitter.

Although things were cruising for me and I was playing well and working hard, there was more adversity after we came back from a spring trip. We were playing Miami of Ohio and, in the first game, I collected two hits in three at-bats. But in game two, I found myself back on the bench. I didn't feel like I deserved to be pulled, and after the game I asked my coach, Fred Decker, why he didn't start me. He told me it was because they didn't want to start a lefty to hit against the left-handed pitcher. I told him that I was 7–11 against lefties so far, a fact he didn't know. The conversation ended and I went home for the night, but I never sat again for the rest of my career at Western Michigan University, even against left-handed pitchers.

Sometimes you have to have the courage to start a conversation that could be uncomfortable. Had I not had that conversation, I may have continued to sit out against left handed pitchers and my future might have ended much differently.

What conversation are you not having that may be holding you back from achieving your goals?

I left as one of WMU's top offensive players in school history, but when the draft came around, I went undrafted and, just like that, my dream of playing in the big leagues hit its biggest-ever road block. My senior year was over, and I had no team to play for, so my career was over. That's when I went to the local independent pro team in town and got a tryout. I made the team and was placed in the starting line-up that same night. After batting practice was over, I went back to my locker, looked at my phone, and saw I'd ten missed calls. One of the calls was from Bob Sullivan, a scout for the Arizona Diamondbacks. I called him right away. Bob said, "Sam, do not play in the game tonight because the Detroit Tigers are going to sign you." I was obviously surprised because Bob wasn't with the Tigers, but he had a friend who was. When the Diamondbacks passed on me in the draft, Bob called in a favor to a friend. I'd had no idea that any of this was happening — I just knew that I was going to get my shot to play professionally *and* I was going to play for the Detroit Tigers, the team that was on my note card! This was the best day of my life.

Guess what? Once I got to Florida to suit up for the Rookie Ball team in Lakeland, the situation became an exact replica as my last two stops. I was a back-up. I started on the bench, then moved to a three-man rotation for two positions, playing two games and sitting one. Trying to adjust to the pro game and playing part-time was extremely difficult, and that showed quickly. After I collected my first hit in my first pro at bat, I only got one more in the next eighteen. I was struggling, so I did what I always did — I kept working, knowing that I would come out of this, and that things would be great because *that is what happens.* I hit for hours, and when they kicked me out of the cage, I lifted. But what ultimately changed my performance was a phone call that cleared my head and reinstated my confidence.

I called Mike Diaz, my former infield and hitting coach at Western Michigan. Mike was, and still is, an amazing guy. We talked, and I told him about my struggles and how it was making me feel. Unlike every other time I'd struggled, this time I was alone. I didn't have family in Lakeland, no friends yet, and the coaches were not very accessible. At the end of the conversation, Mike said, "Dude, what are you worried about? You are going to do what you always do. You will figure it out and start crushing. As a matter of fact you are going to go 15–18 next week." I thanked Mike for his support and said that his confidence meant the world to me.

Who in your life can you turn to when times are tough? Remember, you do not always have to go it alone.

The next day I wasn't supposed to be in the line-up, but I found out that one of the other kids, Eddie Williams, was hurt. How strange that all of my breaks came when someone was injured! But I believe it was my work ethic and continued belief in myself that allowed me to succeed when these opportunities arose. I wasn't lucky — I was prepared when opportunity presented itself.

That week I started every game and went 17–19, which was better than Mike's prediction. When Eddie came back the following week, I'd solidified myself as the lead-off hitter and right fielder. So now, there was a two-man rotation in left field and I played every game. A few weeks later, the stats came out for the league and I was leading the league in hitting. I didn't know it at the time, but there was a future big league all-star named Hanley Ramirez in my league, and I was hitting better than him. I ended the year leading the league in hits and runs scored. This didn't even include the final three weeks of the season because I'd been moved up to a higher league — one of the steps along the way.

Nevertheless, my professional career came to an end three years later, in 2005. I was simply not talented enough to go any further. I had done everything I could to get every ounce of potential out of my body, and it just was not good enough. I had zero potential left. But I could live with that, because I knew the amount of work I put into being the best. I can honestly say that I don't think there was anyone in the world working harder than I was.

The Tale of Cindy Rebman

When I was a personal trainer, a lady name Cindy Rebman (at that time her name was Cindy King), walked into my gym and said she was looking for a trainer. After we talked for a few minutes, Cindy said that her goal was to run a half marathon in five months. This seems like an extremely realistic goal, until you hear the fact that up to and including that day, Cindy had never run a step in her life.

As she was telling me about her dream, she was clearly nervous and full of self-doubt. Her body language was weak, she didn't make eye contact, and she spoke in a soft tone that was very hesitant to say the next word. It almost seemed as if she were waiting for me to kick her out of the gym and tell her she was stupid.

At this point, I didn't know her full story or her **why**, but I could tell that she really wanted to run this race. I also knew I was going to have to convince her it was possible.

As soon as she finished talking, I said, "Let's do this! When do you want to start?" She looked at me in disbelief, as if she were expecting, if not hoping, that I would tell her she was crazy and should start with a 5K or something. But that simply isn't my style. If she wanted to run a half marathon, then that was what she was going to do.

On our first day of training, I put Cindy on a treadmill to see how long she could last. She made it a little over one minute before she had to walk. I wasn't concerned by this because all I wanted to do was give her a baseline so she could see improvement.

But her look was that of complete failure. Of course, I knew better. Her first and most constant form of adversity was her own mind and negative self-talk.

I pushed Cindy through training and I ran with her on training runs. I'm not a huge fan of running, but I did it because she needed it. Two months before the race, Cindy was able to run four miles before she had to walk. We still had a long way to go, but again, I wasn't concerned because she'd already come so far. Cindy was seeing it differently. She was pushing through adversity on a daily basis, but she was still full of self-doubt.

One day we were scheduled to go on a six-mile training run, and I had made my mind up that Cindy was not going to walk at all. On that day, the lesson wasn't about how fast she ran, how she controlled her breathing, or anything related to technique. The lesson on that day was digging deep and pushing herself past what even she thought was possible. To put it simply, the lesson was to **hustle** — to face serious adversity and be persistent.

Cindy tried to walk once, and when I pushed her on her back to let her know it was not happening, she looked at me as if I was trying to kill her. But she kept running. At the end of six miles, Cindy had not walked once. She was breathing heavily, was clearly tired, but she did not walk. When she took her hands off her knees and stood up, I gave her a big hug and told her that we were going to make it.

This was the first time Cindy showed her ability to be persistent, but it would not be her last. On each training run after that, we added distance and she no longer walked. I could see her confidence and belief in herself begin to change. When we started, she dreaded the longest run of the week. After she pushed through all of them, she began to realize that running a half was no longer unrealistic — it was extremely possible!

On race day Cindy was excited and terrified at the same time. She wasn't terrified of failing — she was actually scared of her success because this journey had proven a lot to her about who she was as a person. She was scared because she realized that she would have to keep this confidence up, and at this point in her life, she was not sure it was possible.

I ran this race with Cindy. We were cruising along, not at a record pace, but she was running. She kept running, and as each mile marker passed Cindy began to get a little more emotional. We passed the ten, eleven and twelve mile markers. We were almost there! About a half-mile from the finish line, we encountered a hill. It was a small one, but at this point in the run it looked like Mount Everest. As we approached it, Cindy showed her first weakness of the entire day, telling me, "I can't make it up this hill!" I replied, "Yes, you can," and then I put my hand on her back to let her know that walking was not an option. She had come 12.6 miles of a 13.1-mile race and walking *really was not an option.* Cindy kept running, and it was difficult, but she kept pushing. The pace was slower at this point, but that didn't matter because she was running. When we crossed the finish line, Cindy had completed her journey. She'd run a half marathon.

HUSTLE 'TIL IT HAPPENS

When Cindy started training, she thought running the entire race was unrealistic, and she even mentioned run-walking, but I knew we were going to run this entire race because, not only was it realistic, Cindy needed it for her life. She started training as Cindy King, a scared, out-of-shape person with little confidence. After her divorce was final, she finished the race as Cindy Rebman — a strong, smiling, confident woman who knew the half marathon was just a small step on her life-changing journey. Cindy has since become an avid runner, and has run numerous half marathons. In one recent endeavor, she ran a back-to-back half marathon and full marathon.

Cindy's journey proves that most of the things we think of as unrealistic are simply extremely difficult, and things that are extremely difficult will hurl a ton of adversity at you. If you can handle adversity, you will come out on top every time.

STEP 16: BE PATIENT

So, here you are: you've set an unrealistic goal, created a great process that you've pursued consistently, and you've persisted through a mountain of adversity. Now it's time to relax and be patient.

Although I consider persistence the key factor in achieving success, patience is vitally important because it shows that you have belief. Patience shows that you've let go of the results and have sunk yourself into your process.

Even people that are persistent can get impatient and make decisions that drastically affect their lives. They jump the gun and accept a situation they don't really want. (This is totally different from not being persistent and quitting when things get too tough.) Lacking patience is about being overly eager to claim your prize and taking a sub-par opportunity.

Patience vs. Waiting

2 Chains is a hip hop artist, and in one of his songs he says, "The crazy thing about it, I've knew I had it, I've been being patient, y'all been being stagnant." Later in the song he says, "Labels keep calling I need two mill for this." First of all, we need to address the difference between being patient and waiting. Being patient means you're working hard, going through your process, and continually getting better. Being patient means you have a firm belief in your process, and that what you *really* want is on its way.

> Waiting is the equivalent of sitting on your couch and hoping someone knocks on your door with a job opportunity or a million-dollar check. Waiting lacks action — waiting is being stagnant.
>
> Patience demonstrates the ability to continue moving forward, knowing the opportunity you want is coming.

2 Chains demonstrates his patience in the line about the record labels calling. He says he wants "two mill for this," meaning he wants two million dollars to sign to a label, and he is going to keep sending the labels away until they come up with that amount. This is the essence of patience.

> When you're at the cusp of saying, "I made it," but you're getting offers you're not crazy about, maintain the ability to say, "No thank you." Remember, you have made it this far. What's a little bit longer?

I have a good friend named Mark, who is extremely successful in the pharmaceutical sales field. On more than one occasion, he'd been offered a higher paying job, but it just wasn't the right fit. Mark could have easily taken the money, but he knew the real opportunity he wanted was still out there. He was so confident, that he was willing to pass up a $20,000 raise because the job was simply something he did not want. Most people would have just taken the $20,000 because of the difference it would make in their lives, but Mark's belief system allowed him to remain patient. Two months later, Mark was offered a job that he really wanted, and this time the raise was $60,000 per year.

Throughout his life, Mark displayed extreme competitiveness, consistency, persistence, and, finally, patience. In the end, though, it was the patience that paid off so handsomely for him. I've told Mark's story before, and people ask, "How do you consider him successful when he simply has a job"? I remind them that my idea of success is living the life you intend to live and, as long as I can remember, Mark wanted to live in Chicago and make enough money to do the things he wanted to do without worrying about the bills. This is exactly what he is doing. Mark is the essence of success.

CHOOSE DISCIPLINE AND LIVE LIKE A CHAMPION

The **Hustle 'Til It Happens** program is anchored in the idea that in life, you will suffer two types of pain, and the one you choose will decide your success.

As I sit here at 6:49 a.m. on a chilly Sunday morning in November, I am literally thinking about how I've sacrificed a warm bed in order to get up and create something. I went to bed at 1 a.m. the night before, but by 6:30 a.m. I was fully awake and my mind was running. I had no choice but to wake up and create. Yes, my bed *was* warm, but the thought of staying in it never crossed my mind because if I want to be successful, I know I have to suffer the pain of discipline *or be forced to suffer the pain of regret.*

Suffering the pain of discipline is something I've done my entire life. At this point, it is second nature to me. Although I make sacrifices, they no longer feel like sacrifices. I think of the tasks as simply *what needs to be done.*

When you choose to suffer the pain of discipline, you are choosing a life of success, but the biggest thing you are doing is saying, **"I will get done what needs to be done, when it needs to be done."** If you can live by that quote, your chances of success will magnify by a number you can't even imagine.

Understand, this is scary stuff. Suffering the pain of discipline means giving up things you may enjoy doing now in order to live the life you want to live sometime in the future. Suffering the pain of discipline is scary because, even after all the sacrifices, nothing is guaranteed.

But I can tell you this — if you're a true believer in the **Hustle 'Til It Happens** program, you already understand that *what you want is already happening — it just has not happened YET.*

And what's scarier than not trying? You'll lead a lifetime of "what ifs." Of regret. Of bitterness and envy.

Discipline

> Discipline is defined as "the practice of training people to obey rules or a code of behavior using punishment to correct disobedience." The key words here are **training** and **obey**.

Remember when I told you that my baseball career came to an end because there was no potential left in my body? I had used every ounce of my talent and I was just not good enough. For most people, admitting that would be impossible. Most people would come up with an excuse and blame someone else for their failure and waste a great opportunity to learn.

I have no excuse. I am writing this book right now instead of playing in the big leagues because I simply wasn't good enough to play in the big leagues. I know this because my entire life was dedicated to suffering the pain of discipline. You'll recall that I sacrificed going to parties and snowboarding — I chose the weight room, running sprints in the gym, and throwing. By the time I finished, everyone was already home.

STEP 17: CHOOSE DISCIPLINE

When you choose to suffer the pain of discipline, you do so because it's better than the real punishment in life. The real punishment is never knowing whether you could have accomplished your goal had you given it a decent shot.

By choosing discipline, you're training yourself to create the proper behavior patterns that will increase your chance of success. Noncompliance, in this case, leads to a life of regret.

I looked at hard work and discipline as my friends. I thought they were the two coolest dudes on the block and, therefore, I was able to continue on my path. In high school, when my buddies went on spring break, I stayed home — not because I had to, but because I chose to practice baseball in thirty-degree weather and snow flurries. Sure the beach sounded great, and so did warm sun and girls in bikinis. But what sounded even better was playing games in Comerica Park with 40,000 fans. Staying home didn't guarantee my future, but it guaranteed I had a *chance* at a future.

Life is as much about perception as it is anything else. The way you look at life events shapes your mind-set and, ultimately, your future.

Bill and Smith

When I started giving baseball lessons, I came across kids who *kind of* wanted to play baseball, kids who *loved* to play baseball, and kids who were *playing* only because their dad wanted them to. The latter group of kids is for a different book altogether, but this story is about the other two groups — the one that *really* wants to play baseball and goes all out, and the other group that can't make sacrifices to excel.

101

Here's a story is about a kid named Bill, and a kid we'll call Smith.

Bill was a working machine. He played baseball at any opportunity he could. Bill would go to football practice and immediately afterward, hop the fence and walk to the batting cages to work on improving his game. Bill didn't care what time of day it was, what month it was, or what his friends were doing. He cared about being the absolute best he could be.

Smith was the opposite. Although he would work with me from time to time, he never worked on his game by himself. He did the bare minimum. Smith was a far superior athlete, but it was Bill who went on to play Division I college baseball. Smith's playing days ended with high school.

As they were both hitting one day, Smith was waiting outside the cage to take his turn while Bill was smashing balls off the back of the net. In between one of Bill's swings, Smith said, with a straight face, "If I worked as hard as you do, Bill, I would be way better than you."

As you can imagine, I almost fell over. That one statement summed up the lives of more people around this country and world than anyone can count. That single statement was, and is, being murmured on bar stools throughout the world, in numerous different languages, by millions of different people. I know Smith wanted to play pro baseball, but he was relying on his natural talent to get him there. In my mind, what Smith had really told Bill was, "If I'd been able to suffer the pain of discipline, I wouldn't have to suffer the pain of regret for the rest of my life." I assume that most people feel regret over missing their chance of success.

Muhamad Ali said, "I hated every minute of training, but I said 'don't quit. Suffer now and live the rest of your life as a champion.'" That quote is the essence of discipline.

Suffering requires great discipline. By definition, it means to experience or be subjected to something bad or unpleasant. Discipline is wanting something so badly that you're willing to put yourself through "something bad or unpleasant."

Remember, nobody told Ali he had to train, nobody told him he had to keep going. Ali made a conscious decision to suffer the pain of discipline because he knew that anything less would lead to a life of regret.

There are two quotes from Michael Jordan that also explain suffering the pain of discipline. Jordan said, "I can accept failure, everyone fails at something, but I can't accept not trying." This quote speaks to the heart of discipline. Yes, we know we might not make it, we know nothing is guaranteed, but in the **Hustle 'Til It Happens** program, our thoughts, process, discipline, and work ethic are so ingrained in us that we stay fiercely focused on getting better every time the clock ticks.

Jordan also said, "I'm not out there sweating for three hours every day just to find out what it feels like to sweat." I love this quote because you can hear the disbelief in his tone, that people don't understand the passion and focus it takes to become great. You can actually see the wheels in his head spinning, as if he were really saying, *is there any other option than to put 100 percent of yourself in to get the very thing you want most out of this world?* The answer to that question would be "No," there is simply no other option.

You owe it to your future self to work hard now so your future self can lie down at night and rest peacefully, knowing there are no "what ifs."

J.J. Watt is a defensive end for the Houston Texans. Before the 2014 NFL season, Watt signed a deal worth $100 million. The morning after Watt signed this record-breaking deal, he was in the weight room at 4 a.m. Most people would think, "Why? That's crazy! You're rich. Relax and sleep in, and enjoy your money." This is why most people never achieve the level of success they are capable of. J.J. Watt didn't get a $100 million contract because he chose to sleep in or take days off. That contract came because he *was willing* to lift at 4 a.m. when everyone else was sleeping.

Matt Loomis

Matt Loomis is a former player, turned friend. Matt was a crafty lefty, meaning he didn't throw very hard, but he was able to find success on the mound — enough success to play in college. But Matt's collegiate baseball career ended after three years. By that time, he had decided on becoming a dentist. It would take two more years of undergraduate classes, but Matt's resolve was locked and loaded. He didn't waver in his ambition — but to be honest, his resolve had not really and truly been tested.

During the course of his undergrad program, Matt had to take a test just to be able to apply to dental school. He and I talked on a regular basis and he was excited about the upcoming challenge — but he knew it was going to be a serious challenge. Outside of going to school, he also had to work in order to afford his apartment, groceries, car, and phone bill. The job that was not conducive to getting in proper study time, so Matt decided to make a schedule change. He decided to wake up at 4 a.m., go to work until 9:30 a.m., head home to grab some food, then go to classes and study at the library at Central Michigan University until it closed at 10 p.m.

At this point in his life, Matt was twenty-three. He knew he had to make the sacrifice. During a phone conversation, he actually told me, "The guys can't understand why I put myself through this. They think I'm crazy to put these hours in, but, like I told one of them, 'In fifteen years, I'll be a dentist living in California, and you will still be here wishing you did something besides party.'" It wasn't as though that statement was a revelation to me — Matt had always been a little wiser than his buddies — but it was still impressive. What happened next is the most unbelievable part of the story.

Test day comes and goes. Matt has to wait for his results to come back, but in the interim he tells me how he was prepared as he possibly could be, and it was the toughest test he had ever taken. He recounted the two straight months he'd spent in the library, not talking to any of his friends. He recalled always being tired, but never really being tired because the dream in his head was so huge that it kept him awake. Then Matt got his results — and he'd failed. As he explains it, he was crushed. He'd spent five years of his life working toward passing this test — and getting into dental school — and it all came crashing down. It was not that he couldn't take the test again — it was the sacrifices he'd made ... and then to get such a low score.

At this point, most people would have chosen an average path, they would have finished up with a lesser degree and gotten a job they didn't want to do — a job they'd hate for the rest of their lives. But the pursuit of a worthy ideal makes life worth living, and Matt knew this. After he got his test scores back on Friday, he was back in the library on Monday. He chose to stay the course and stay disciplined. He realized that *you never fail until you quit, and the pain of giving up hurts way more than trying.* Matt was back to hustling, and more determined — and focused — than ever before.

Matt understands the concept of suffering the pain of discipline and, as I write this book, I can guarantee that Matt is either in one of his dental classes at the University of Michigan or in the library taking care of business. Matt's story embodies all the qualities of the **Hustle 'Til It Happens** program. Like all the other people I write about in this book, Matt followed the steps, believed in the process, and kept moving forward on a daily basis.

If more people were willing to suffer the pain of discipline, the phrase would be used in a much more positive light than it usually is. The fact is, most people will remove themselves from the equation. Most people are unwilling to put themselves through pain and discomfort and will, therefore, remain average.

You cannot achieve your dreams without the ability to suffer the pain of discipline. It simply will not happen.

SEE IT, THEN BECOME IT

Visualization allows you to see things that have not yet happened, which gives you a sense of confidence and success that you could only otherwise create by the actual doing.

People will argue that you can't have success without confidence, and others will say you can't have confidence until you've had success. I argue that you can create both in your mind before they ever happen in real life and, therefore, there is no argument about which comes first. The only discussion left is, **are you going to put this key piece of the puzzle into action.**

As a young kid — just like a lot of young kids — I had a fear of the dark. But unlike most kids, the fear never really left me. At age twelve, I remember lying in my bed in Lexington, Kentucky, not able to sleep because I was scared from a TV show or a thought that had entered my head. Later in life, I would realize that this fear came from moving around so much and a lack of stability. It took me until the age of thirty-three before I became comfortable sleeping in a house by myself, in my bed, with all the lights off. I tell you this not to embarrass myself, but because there was only one thought growing up that could ease this deep fear. If I closed my eyes and imagined playing baseball in Tiger Stadium, I could fall asleep.

I'd been to a few games, so I knew the layout like the back of my hand. But the stadium was just the beginning. I could hear the fans cheering, I could smell the popcorn and feel the excitement as the crowd hollered and screamed and stamped their feet. I would stand in the box with two out, two strikes, and the bases loaded in game seven of the World Series. And then I would hit it out of the park.

Because I was scared pretty much every night — sometimes to the point of crawling under my parents' bed — I would imagine this scenario on a nightly basis. It was not until many years later that I learned this was actually called *visualization*, and it could help improve performance in *any area of life*.

As I grew up, I never studied or watched videos on how visualization could help athletic performance — it was just something I continued to do because when I visualized, *I felt the feeling of success*. Later in my baseball career, I found myself in some very intense situations as a hitter, and can honestly say that I only remember two times when I failed to produce a hit. Both of those times, I hit the balls to the fence and the fielder made a great play. This is not ego, trust me. I could bore you with the details of my game-winning home runs, but I'll just make it short. I hit those home runs just the way I'd imagined I would every night of my life as a kid growing up. I believe my early visualization set me up for success later, and in life, and I now teach visualization as a success tool.

My childhood visualization sessions were not an attempt to improve my athletic ability or create a better swing, they were simply to help me relax and fall asleep. The funny thing was, at the age of twelve I was creating habits that would literally carry me into professional baseball.

Remember, I said I was just trying to relax and go to sleep. All the examples above were high-pressure situations. The thing about every one of those situations is that I felt *zero pressure* and was never even a little nervous. And this was not me blocking out the feelings.

What really happened — without me knowing it — was my visualization skills took over, and I was able to relax and do in real life what I'd always done in my visualization sessions — hit home runs. I did not actively recall my visualization sessions or even the feeling they created, but because I'd been in the home-run-hitting situation thousands of times in my mind, when it happened in real life, I was relaxed and ready to do my job.

Why use a story of unintentional results? I use the story because I want you to imagine the success you can and will have when you add intention to your visualization program.

Powerful Mind

I'll get to the scientific evidence, but first I want to share a story that I suspect has happened to you numerous times in your life. How do I know? Simple. It happens to all of us *because our minds are powerful.*

Remember back to a time you had a disagreement with someone. This disagreement was not simply about who got to ride in the front seat — think instead about an argument that was important to you. Do you remember what you did after you left the location of the disagreement and you were in your own space (for me this is almost always the shower)?

So you are in your own space (shower, car, room) and you begin to replay the disagreement in your head. You begin to think about the things you wished you *would have said.* As you remember things the other person did say, you begin to amend the (now historical) disagreement with your new statements. Your heart rate picks up, your adrenaline starts pumping, and before you know it, you are right back in the middle of the disagreement with the exact same feelings and emotions. This is visualization at its finest.

Replaying a disagreement, argument, or fight in our heads is probably the most common form of **unintentional visualization** — and that is a shame. I say that because it's not all that helpful to replay a disagreement unless you **consciously try to learn** from it. Without the learning, you've used a powerful tool for nothing at all.

Why is visualization so powerful? It's powerful because *your mind doesn't know that your body is not actually performing the action*. Your brain can't distinguish between *a thought of performing* an action, or if you are *actually performing* the action. Brain scans have shown that a person imagining herself playing a piano activates almost the exact same networks of neurons as a person actually playing the piano.

Alan Richardson, an Australian psychologist, set out to prove how much better we can become with the intentional use of our mind. Richardson split a team of basketball players into three groups, then tested each player's ability to shoot free throws.

Group 1 shot free throws for twenty minutes per day

Group 2 only visualized themselves making free throws, they did not actually shoot

Group 3 did not practice or visualize

The group that visualized made significant gains and their results were almost the same as the group that actually practiced. I know that "almost" might make you skeptical, but remember, the group *never touched a ball* and they still improved a great deal because their neurons fired in almost the exact same fashion as the group that actually shot. This puts them far ahead when they actually do start shooting.

First-person Visualization

Think of first-person visualization as a movie. You're not watching the scene, you are an actor **performing** in the scene.

I've found this form of visualization to be the most effective: I feel emotions more intensely when I'm actually *in the scene*. The crowd reacts, and tensions grow and I am the one creating the tension, so I'm able to react with strong emotional connections. I am a competitor. My heart begins to race and my adrenaline kicks in. My subconscious mind sees this image as real, because *I am actually doing it.*

Again, with visualization, your mind *does not know* that your body is not performing. As your subconscious mind records these images, they begin to feel real. The more real they feel, the more confident you become because you've accomplished what you wanted to.

> I'm not telling you, "Visualize and you will receive." I am telling you to "Visualize in order to create confidence, then **hustle** to go get the dream your subconscious mind already owns."

Another plus: the visualization has connected your brain to your body in a way that will make learning quicker once you begin to practice. As my friend Alan Jaeger says, "Neurons that fire together, wire together."

Third-person Visualization

Third-person visualization is also like watching a movie, only you're watching yourself from a distance. This kind of visualization can help you see an action that you've never performed before. Think of this as teaching yourself how to do the actions **before** you actually do them.

For example, you could visualize watching yourself open the doors to your new business. Since you've never done it before, seeing it in the third-person *first* can really help create the entire scene. You are able to see other businesses on the block, people walking by your store, and you can see how you mingle and interact with the people that come through your open doors. In this form of visualization, you get to sit back and enjoy a movie you are creating and watching. Third-person visualization doesn't create the same intense emotions as first-person visualization, but it does help set a scene, which is why I encourage my clients to use both.

Again, put more emphasis on first-person visualization because it creates more intense emotions, and emotions are a huge piece in the ultimate success of visualization.

I mostly use first-person visualization these days because I am trying to accomplish things I've already done, only on a bigger scale. I don't need to see what it looks like first, because I already know. But often, when I'm having a hard time getting into my first-person state, I will actually start with third-person in order to set the scene. Once I've got that, and I can see myself in the scene, I let my mind slow down and focus better. I then break state — meaning I open my eyes and leave the scene altogether — then I focus on my breathing to get back into the scene, but now I can do it in the first person and much quicker.

High-pressure Visualization

One technique to enhance performance during actual high-pressure, fast-moving situations is to quickly get into this third-person scene-making visualization. Creating a mental image as fast as you can in a pressure situation will allow you to relax and focus. Once you leave the visualization, you'll enter back into the present moment with confidence.

This won't be something you can do without practice, but here's how it works: Imagine a scene in which you've already been successful and where there was also pressure to perform. Use a specific moment from the past that matches, as closely as possible, the specific moment in the present.

For example, if a baseball player wants to get better at two-strike hitting (they all do), I coach them to use a scene in which they were already successful with two strikes. If a sales person wants to get better at closing sales in a room with multiple people — instead of just being good at one-on-one sales — I will have them visualize a time they were successful in that situation.

STEP 18: VISUALIZE

To practice, first select a successful scene from the past that you think can help performance in the future. I want you to get into the scene and use all of your senses and allow it to create emotion. Now, quickly break state and go do something else: walk around your house, watch TV, make food, etc.

After a few minutes, return to your quiet place and quickly get back into the scene. You will more than likely find this to be tough going, and that's because it is. High-pressure visualization takes practice, and lots of it. If you can't get right back into the scene, keep working on it.

Why is this so important to your success? Because high-pressure visualization is just what you'll need in the high pressure of competition.

If you have two strikes — and you need to relax — you only have a few seconds to get your mind right. You must be able to quickly find that mental success, then open your eyes and get ready to compete.

Or maybe you're walking toward the door, getting ready to make a sales pitch to a crowd of people. Suddenly, a rush of anxiety hits you. You don't have time to lie down and take ten minutes to breathe and visualize. You'll need to *immediately visualize* a positive scene that exactly reflects the one you're walking into.

You can do this. It just takes practice. With practice you'll be able to control your breathing, visualize positive results, and give yourself the best possible chance of succeeding.

Mental Block

Sometimes, a person has such a mental block with a certain situation that instead of trying to get them to visualize the exact scene, I get them visualize something completely unrelated.

A few years ago I worked with Cooper, who is now playing Division I Baseball at Western Michigan University. In high school Cooper simply could not get over his fear of striking out. Because of this, he would lock up and not swing at all. I tried a number of different techniques and nothing worked. Finally, we started working on his "happy place."

I had Cooper think about and write down the moment in his life when he remembered just having fun and being completely happy — it didn't matter that Cooper's "happy place" had nothing to do with baseball. For Cooper, "happy" was a place with a bunch of friends on a lake, and they were tubing behind the boat piloted by his buddy's dad. He remembered an immense feeling of happiness and joy.

I had him visualize that place, and he was really able to lock in on his exact emotions. We practiced the techniques I describe above to quickly get him into that scene for a two-strike game situation. We knew he'd only have a few seconds to find it and relax.

Cooper had tremendous success with this and other visualization skills. He went on to have an amazing summer in which he hit five home runs and caught the eye of both college and pro scouts. He was later offered a Division I baseball scholarship, but he turned it down and accepted an offer to Kellogg Community College because he thought it was a better fit. After two years at Kellogg he accepted an offer to play at Western Michigan, as I mentioned above.

I have used this exact same technique with people who have later implemented it in unexpected areas of their lives. For example, I got a phone call from a young man telling me he used his visualization skills to help him relax and pass his driver's training test. Another young man told me he put them to use before he took the ACT.

One of my favorite stories is about John. John would continually let others control his emotions with their actions until we finally connected for one-hour conversations, once per week. John used visualization and breathing skills (next chapter) to relax and completely change his reactions to stressful situations, particularly during a messy break-up with the mother of his child. He put visualization and breathing skills to work in order for him to not react to negativity, but instead, to let it roll off his shoulders. This was difficult for him because his upbringing was extremely confrontational — it was bred into him to attack at every opportunity. Within one month of telephone coaching though, John was able to control his emotions and let go of the things he had no control over. It was truly an amazing experience to witness. John has since moved on and is extremely happy in a new relationship with a person he attracted into his life due to his positive mindset.

Visualization is a step in the **Hustle 'Til It Happens** program that you should use on a daily basis. To maximize your visualization results, you will need to be intentional, practice proper breathing techniques — which I'll describe next — infuse the emotions you're feeling, and find a quiet place so you can focus and be completely relaxed.

BREATHE TO BE BETTER

Conscious breathing means you are using your breath for a purpose — to let go of stress, increase the amount of oxygenated blood to your brain and muscles, and to bring yourself back to the moment.

The concept sounds so simple. Breathe. I know you're thinking you already do this — and you are correct — but I want to focus on *conscious breathing* in order to improve your overall ability to perform at a high level. Conscious breathing is for athletes, entrepreneurs, stay-at-home moms or dads — really any person that needs to learn to relax, be present, and create discipline or confidence in order to improve — basically all of us.

Breathing is natural, but taking deep, cleansing breaths for better performance when we are anxious is not natural. In fact, it's the opposite of natural. Usually, our breaths become shallow and quick when we get into high-stress situations, like a sales pitch to a Fortune 500 company, a speaking gig, or a job interview. The problem is, when we take quick, shallow breaths, we actually create *more* anxiety because we're not getting proper blood flow. Shallow breaths deprive our muscles of much needed oxygen, and without sufficient oxygen, our body cannot perform up to its standards in pressure, or even non-pressure situations. Shallow breathing can also happen as we get older, if we don't practice proper techniques.

The solution is breathing from your diaphragm, the dome-shaped muscle that lies just above your stomach cavity. Using your diaphragm muscle allows you to fully empty and fill your lungs, creating blood flow that's rich in oxygen, leading to relaxation and a return to the moment.

For athletes, you're also increasing endurance by allowing the body to convert fuel to energy. As a baseball coach, I would always hear other coaches yell to their kids, "JUST RELAX!!!" This always made me laugh, simply because the team had never practiced relaxing and yelling at someone doesn't exactly instill a sense of calmness. So, here you have this poor kid, nervous about the situation at hand, and now reaching the height of anxiety because the coach is yelling for him to do something he has no idea how to do.

STEP 19: JUST BREATHE

Proper breathing takes practice, and you'll need to do a few different things in order to make it happen.

First, you must learn the breathing technique.

Second, you must strengthen the muscles (diaphragm and intercostal).

Third, you must practice this daily, or even multiple times per day, so that proper breathing becomes natural.

Exercise:

To test whether or not you breathe correctly, lie back, place your hand on your stomach, and breathe normally. If your hand is moving a good amount, you are stomach breathing. If not, you are chest breathing. Chest breathing (shallow breathing) is what we want to avoid.

Now, you'll have to focus. Still reclining, take a breath that fills up your stomach and expands your rib cage.

Release.

Continue to do this until you notice a pulling in your abdominal cavity. When you feel that, you are actually using diaphragmatic breathing by activating the external, intercostal muscles. These muscles are responsible for raising the rib cage and expanding the chest cavity as you take deep breathes or forced inhalations.

The intercostal muscles are extremely important to increasing performance, but very rarely get the strengthening they need. One way to strengthen them is to practice deep breathing on a daily basis.

Deep Breathing Exercise

Lie on your back, place your hands across your stomach, bend your knees, your feet flat on the floor. Inhale deeply for a two-count, hold for a two-count, and exhale for a four-count. Doing this not only strengthens the muscles, it relaxes you as well.

Intercostal muscles can also be strengthened with twisting or bending exercises that stretch and strengthen. Sit ups that require you to extend backward past parallel to the ground are effective as well.

Life Breath

Throughout this book, you've heard me talk again and again about breathing and focusing on your breathing. Now I want to take it a step further: **I want you to become your breath**. Proper breathing will increase your ability to stay in the moment, it will increase your ability to relax, gain confidence, compete, concentrate, be disciplined, and it will help your visualizing skills immensely.

There is a good reason I put this section this far back in the book. A lot of people have a hard time buying into this technique, but if you're still reading my book, I assume I have your trust. If I do, I hope you will take this part seriously because proper breathing will enhance everything you do in life.

As with any other skill, you must give breathing the proper practice in order for it to be effective. As a society, we tend to deny breath work because we are so concerned with the physical work — the doing. But breathing practice is natural and primordial, and will create a better physical performance if you practice it daily.

Breathing Practice

Start with ten minutes per day. Yes, ten minutes of focused silence, just you and your breath.

As you can imagine, I get a lot of push-back from clients when I ask them to be quiet and calm for ten minutes. Why? Because they are busy and this does not seem like a priority. But after one week of practice, they invariably notice a difference. And after four weeks, they cannot go on without getting their ten quiet minutes per day.

Become the Breath

Bring your attention to the diaphragm by placing your hand on your stomach. Breathing through your nose, you will begin the inhalation phase of your breath from the diaphragm. Understand, there isn't a right or wrong amount of oxygen to inhale, just breathe for now. Remember also to exhale through your nose.

Your job is to watch the breath do the work. I want you to actually see the air coming in through your nose and filling up your lungs. Then, I want you to watch as it exits the body during the exhalation phase.

You are no longer breathing when you are doing this, you are **becoming the breath**, and when you become the breath, you are present.

Do this exercise for three minutes.

Remember, at this point there is no specific timing to the breathing sequence. Just become the breath. What we're trying to do is get to a place where you are *not thinking*. If any non-breathing thoughts enter your head, stop, re-focus, and breathe.

Cadence Breathing

The next phase is cadence breathing. This is not the same "cadence breathing" that runners use, although the idea is the same. Runners will use foot strikes to trigger an inhale or an exhale, effectively creating a timed breathing mechanism in order to improve performance. Since you will not be running, but rather lying on your back, there will be a predetermined cadence.

Cadence Breathing

Start by inhaling for a two-count, hold for a three-count, and exhale for a six-count. Just like before, focus on your diaphragm.

In the hold phase, make sure to stay relaxed. My clients tend to squeeze or tense up when they first start, and it's important to loosen up and just let the breath sit.

For the exhale, remember that it happens through your nose.

Repeat this for a total of four minutes.

Back to the Breath

After the cadence breathing, go back to the first step and become the breath again. There is no more counting, just breathing for three minutes at a comfortable pace — in through the nose and out the same way.

It is important to understand that although this is a ten-minute exercise, you may feel so good that you'll want to stay with it a little longer. If that happens, great! Just continue until you are ready to finish.

Take ten minutes right now to practice.

When you first start out, you'll want to find a quiet place, away from distractions. Eventually, you will be able to do this in the middle of

Times Square, in a board room, on an athletic field, or even right before you head on stage to deliver the best talk of your life.

Visualization and Breath

Throughout the visualization chapter, I asked you to focus on your breath, then get into your visualizing. I recommend this whenever possible because it allows your breath to become a reminder, and in the middle of a stressful situation, reminders are important.

As you visualize and focus on your breath, relate your breath to your mental picture. In this way, you're creating muscle memory which you can activate in live competition. Remember the neurons fire in almost exactly the same way during visualization as they do during action. Breathing properly during visualization is effectively tying the visualized activity to your breath.

All of my clients are taught to take a deep breath before any stressful or threatening situation — also before non-stressful situations. My pitchers take a deep breath before each pitch, not just the bases-loaded pitches. Again, doing this creates priority and muscle memory. Taking a deep breath before every pitch makes it routine and part of the process. The experienced players do it without even thinking about it. When they get into a stressful situation, they simply rely on their training.

I work on this same technique with people who are in stressful relationships. John, whom you met earlier, was taught to deeply breathe before, during, and after he inserts himself into a situation that he suspects may turn toxic.

Of course, we can't always avoid stress, or even toxic situations, but we can and should prepare for them. Practicing our breathing is the very best way to get prepared. As Alan Jaeger says, "The breath is always happening now. It serves as a reminder to come back to this moment, this action; being present is a huge part of being process oriented."

GET YOUR MIND RIGHT

A strong mental game takes practice. Whether you are aspiring to be a top-notch athlete, a business owner, salesman, good friend, or a great wife or husband, your mental game is going to have to be strong.

We have already talked about visualization and breathing techniques, now we're going to touch on the most important technique of all: **getting your mind right**. Thoughts can either tear you down or take you to the next level. But here's the secret: in order to think properly, **we must be active listeners to our own thoughts.**

I went out for a run one day and, mind you, despite the half marathon story earlier, I am not much of a runner. I usually do it just to prove to myself that I am still very much a competitor.

My normal runs end right around three miles, but on this day I was going to go five. I set it in my mind that five was the distance I was going to run, and I took off out of my driveway. As always, the run started out great. My breathing was good, my pace was solid, and my legs were fresh. I use the app, Map My Run, and at every mile the voice would announce the pace, time, and distance traveled over my headphones. After one mile, I was cruising and feeling great. When I crossed the two-mile mark, my pace was strong and my breathing steady. But the closer I got to three miles, the more my mind started to think I had already succeeded, and it actually began to tell me to stop.

As the voice came over my headphones, "Distance, three miles, pace 7:45, time, 23:15," my mind said, "Nice work, great run, you should be proud of yourself, you can stop now." A few more paces and my mind said, "This is actually my best pace in the last three runs over the last month. You can stop now."

I'm telling you my mind was talking to me because it was. We all talk to ourselves, all day, and if we could put a tape recorder on those thoughts, we might be embarrassed about the way we treat ourselves.

On this day, I hadn't heard the last of him. That voice was extremely negative in a positive way.

Sound weird? It was. My voice was patronizing me. It was trying to keep me from putting my body through any more stress, and it was doing it by telling me I had already accomplished enough.

I have actually named my voice: I call him Samson. I even gave him a physical body to make him feel real. I encourage you to do the same.

At around the three and a half mile mark, I saw my voice sitting on a bench. He was encouraging me to sit next to him, take a break, and relax. The one thing you should know about me is that once I put a number in my head — for a run or cardio session — that number gets completed. Although my voice knows this, it never stops trying to sabotage me. I ran past the bench and said, "I'll see you at home. I have to finish this run."

At four miles, when I got my report, my legs were burning, my chest was burning, and my breathing was getting ragged. I was way past my comfort threshold with the pace, but I was running.

Then, sure enough, there he was again. This time my voice was standing in the middle of the sidewalk demanding that I stop. He said, "That's enough. This hurts! We cannot go any further."

But it was too late. Yes, I was exhausted, but I just said, "Excuse me, I have to finish."

That was the last time I heard from the voice on this particular run, but it wasn't the last time I had to talk to myself.

At four and half miles, I was in pain. My legs were burning, I could taste blood, I was trying hard to control my breathing. This was the hardest part of the course due to the steady, although not steep, up-hill climb. As my mind began to focus on the pain and how far I still had to go, I saw an elderly man who was barely able to walk. He was moving slowly, his body leaning to the right, his left shoulder slightly higher than his right. Although I was tired, I clearly saw every detail of his struggle. He was hunched over and not able to extend his neck, in other words, he was always looking at the ground from a forty-five degree angle.

This man's struggle — and courage — completely changed my mind-set. For the entire run, I had been telling my voice I had to finish the run. But watching this man struggle to just barely walk, I realized I do not *have* to finish, I *get* to finish.

I'm sure the guy was grateful to be outside and walking, but I'm also sure he'd like to stand up straight and move with ease. I thought to myself, "How lucky are you?" I truly had this thought, and, all of a sudden, I got a second wind. I focused on my breathing more than I did the finish line. I narrowed my focus to the next step, realizing that if I just kept taking the next step, I would reach the finish line. I was still tired, but I chose to focus on how fortunate I was to be able to run. I finished the five miles, and I realized — more so than ever — that my mental game training and positive perspective had carried me just as much as my legs.

Nobody is excluded from having negative thoughts. My journey to professional baseball, becoming a paid speaker, and now a real estate agent was, and is, full of stories like the one above. There were times during my journeys when I thought, "Enough is enough, just take the easy route." Or, "Go back to school and get a job." These times were almost exclusively when I was in a bad state — tired, hungry, just had a speaking gig or one of my deals fall through. The difference between successful people and those that veer off the intended path is their ability to control these thoughts and get back to a positive state.

The story of my run is 100 percent true, although it wasn't life or death, or even a possible career-ender. The story reflects the mind-set it takes to push through adversity in any situation. The story of my run details numerous skills I work on daily in order to improve performance.

STEP 20: RECOGNIZE, REPLACE, REPEAT

You know the voice. It's the one that says, "Do not screw up" ... "I hope I don't fail" ... "It probably won't work out this time" ... "I'll start my diet tomorrow" ... "You're too old to be doing this."

This is the negative voice. We all have one, and in order to be successful, we must acknowledge that fact before we can move on. If we try to ignore the voice, he or she will win. The negative voice exists and now it is time to learn how to deal with it.

It doesn't matter what self-defeating statement your negative voice makes, it just matters that we recognize it's talking. So step one is, **Recognize the negative voice.** Acknowledge the voice when it's talking and listen to what it's saying.

This takes practice, and a good starting point — one that I used with my clients — is to write down a list of what the voice says and in what kind of situation(s) it speaks. Do this over a few days so that you're listening and noticing when it speaks to you. Recognizing the situations when you hear the voice will give the voice context. And once you have context, you'll be prepared to deal with it. You'll know exactly when the voice is likely to pop up and try to tear you down. This list is never short, and the words spoken are never encouraging. But the good news is, now that you hear it, you can stop it.

Now that we've recognized and documented the when and where, we can move to the next part: replacing the negative voice with a positive thought. This thought can be any thought, but it will usually be one that counters the voice's current opinion of you. If the voice says, "You suck, you cannot accomplish this task," you must counter and counter quickly ... before the voice mounts a full-fledged attack.

Exercise:

Recall a time when you had success. Use visualization. Breath. Talk back to your negative voice.

Your negative voice doesn't hate you. *It's actually trying to keep you safe from embarrassment and pain and failure.* But remember, living a life we never intended to live is more embarrassing and painful than any amount of failure will ever be.

Another way of countering the negative voice is to recognize how you are **feeling**. Recognize your current state.

For example, my negative voice will say, "Give up. You are stupid. Be realistic." I will quickly assess my current state and reply, "No, I am not stupid. I am just really hungry and tired. I'll no longer try to be productive until the problem is solved."

Understanding your current state is like your auto-reply for email. When you're out of the office and you get an email, the email application tells the sender when you'll be back.

Understanding and being in touch with your current state can help you have an auto-reply to the negative voice.

Defining Success, Again

Here's another reason to listen to **when** your negative voice speaks, not just **what** he is saying. A lot of people don't give themselves enough credit for the success they've had in life. Society has basically taught us not to count our success unless it is huge: an author is not a success unless she is a best-selling author, an entrepreneur is not a success unless he's a millionaire, a baseball player is not a success unless he makes the big leagues. This view helps our negative voice gain many victories over us.

So, let's begin to appreciate success for what it is. That author is a success because she had the courage to sit down and begin, and not only begin, but see the book through. If you got up today without hitting the snooze button, you are a winner to me. If you crawled out of your warm bed and went to the gym when you really didn't want to, you're a champion. If you promised yourself a three-mile walk in the morning and you woke up and did just that, I say, "Congrats. That is a success."

I don't care about the amount of money you have, or if there are news articles touting your success. What makes you successful is if you are doing what you intended to do with your life and follow through on the promises you've made yourself.

We need to count our successes daily — it's a vitally important step for our mental health. The world tends to tell you what we've done wrong, not right. The world condemns our unrealistic goals. Our negative voice will chime in as well. But if we keep track of our successes, we not only have a chance, but we can ultimately win the battle of negativity and come out the other side, successful and happy. Remember, success is ours to define, and when we take that power back, we are taking control of our lives.

Practice!

Now that you've recognized your negative voice, and are able to combat it with the positive thoughts — practice! Practice on a daily basis. The system goes as follows: **recognize, replace, and repeat**. After a while your practice will make them a natural part of who you are.

Until that time, though, you must actively participate in this step and take notes along the way. I know this may seem overwhelming right now, but this very step alone will change the way you view yourself. And when you change the way you view yourself, then and only then will you be able to unleash your greatness upon the world.

Exercise:

Before we go any further, I'd like you to put a bookmark on this page. Set the book down, get out a piece of paper and give your negative voice a name. This is not a joke. Giving your voice a name will make it real, and it's easier to do battle when your enemy is real.

Write the name down, and anytime you have dialogue with your negative voice, call it by its name. With a name, the voice no longer is a thought. It becomes a person who is treating you in a way that you do not allow people to treat you.

One more thing, it is inadvisable to stand around and have a conversation — by name — with your voice at a bus stop. This conversation usually takes place in your head. However, I will tell you for a fact that I've had some pretty awesome conversations with my voice out loud in the safety and comfort of my own home.

START A POSITIVITY JOURNAL

Now it's time to build your responses and create more confidence than you ever thought possible. You are going to start a journal to document positive thoughts and feelings about yourself.

STEP 21: TALK BACK

This journal will consist of three parts. You may find it helpful to draw two lines on each page of your journal to make three columns or sections. The three parts are:

→ Something you like about yourself

→ Something you are good at

→ Your most recent success

This journal won't squash your negative voice altogether, but it will give you the tools you need to fight back quickly and effectively.

Start your journaling by writing down three items for each one of the above criteria. After that, it would be beneficial to add one entry in each column daily — and three would be awesome!

I admit that I've had a few clients who've felt overwhelmed by journaling seven days a week. Since the idea of this exercise is to create confidence and build you up, feel free to schedule it to fit your lifestyle. Even if you only journal three times a week, you're still gaining nine positive thoughts that you didn't have before. This is a marathon, not a sprint, and this exercise is going to build your confidence in the present. By building your confidence in the present, you are giving yourself tools for the future.

Something You Like About Yourself

This could be as simple as how your jeans fit today.

Your jeans fitting the way you like is not really a simple thought at all when you drill down. If your jeans fit great today, that means the effort and hard work you have been putting in is paying off, which in turn makes your jeans fitting today a recent success.

Something you like about yourself could also be the skillful way that you handled rude customers. Again, this will cause you to think: handling a rude customer is a skill, and it takes patience. What does the way you handle rude customers say about how great of a person you are?

Also, it's okay, and very much encouraged, to think of yourself as **GREAT**. As a matter of fact, it is almost a necessity. You do not have to say these words out loud to other people, but say them to yourself: "I am great, look at how I handled that person who was being rude on purpose." The list of what you can write down in the journal is endless. Just start writing.

Something You Are Good At

Maybe you make great scrambled eggs, or maybe you're skilled at writing a business plan, or you could be really good at organization, or helping others get organized.

One lady I met with told me she was good at creating workout plans for her clients. And she was also very good at sex. After I stopped myself from spitting out my coffee, I thought, "That does count."

Again, the only thing that really matters in this exercise is that you define what "good" means to you and you write it down. You never know what might turn up. If you're good at helping other people get organized, it's possible that that particular journal entry may start a new career path for you. People will pay a lot of money for someone who can de-clutter their life and make them more efficient.

A Recent Success

Write down something that you've recently done well. Go ahead — it isn't that hard, and you get to define success.

Remember the alarm clock? If you woke up today without hitting the snooze button, you've got a success. If you wrote one chapter of a book, or you created a new recipe, or you finished your homework, or you went an entire day without swearing, that's success.

The first time we defined success in this book, it pertained to your dream goal. This time, it's about small, daily successes that will ultimately build massive confidence and give your the ability to tell your negative voice to kick rocks.

The final step is to take one of the items you wrote down and actually journal about it. This will mean writing one or two paragraphs, or more if you choose.

Again, I don't want the process to overwhelm you, but this step is important because it's a concrete paragraph or two of you telling yourself everything positive about yourself. You'll find it's empowering.

As an example, take your recent success of not hitting the snooze button. You can write about the fact it made you feel like your life was on the right track. You can talk about how it made you feel excited about the day, and the future, because you no longer wanted to just lie in bed. You wanted to get up and start creating the life you intended to live.

The Toxic Voice

Even after we get out of our own way, there are still going to be outside distractions, negativity, and interference that will make us question ourselves. Some people call this "hating," or the people that do it, "haters," but I choose to look at them as uninformed.

Calling these people "uninformed" gives them the benefit of the doubt. They may not know what's possible, what's already been done, and how a positive mind-set and work ethic can make it all come true. They do not know ... **YET.**

I also know that uninformed people surely cannot be right about a situation they know nothing about. Plus, it's an opportunity to teach, and I love to teach.

There's no doubt that if your dream is bold enough — "unrealistic" enough — you'll have plenty of people tell you it's impossible. More often than not, these people are family members or friends. One thing you must do before you call them "haters," or "stupid," or even block them out, is to look at *their* life. Look at what they are doing. Not to judge them, but to try and understand why they are saying what they are saying. If they've never chased a dream, or never set a goal for an intended life, it's no wonder they don't understand your mission. If they've failed, then they may want you to fail, too. Misery loves company.

I strongly encourage you to take the time to talk to these people. After all, they are friends and family. Talk to them about what you are doing, and explain to them that their support would be wonderful. But here comes the hard part: *Let them know that if they are not going to be supportive, you are going to have to remove yourself from their lives.* Let them know that you understand that they don't have the same mission or goal as you do, but there is no way that you are going to stand around and let them derail your dreams with their negativity. You have now given them a choice, and that is all anyone can ask. You've not told them you are done with them; you've simply given them a choice.

Now, it is time to surround yourself with people with the same mind-set and work ethic as you. It's nice to have friends who match the size of your dream.

Control What You Can Control

It's also extremely important to understand that you, too, always have a choice. The most important choice you have is to control only the things that you can control. This choice will take you further in life than any other choice you can make. Why? Because it gives you freedom. Controlling what you can control gives you the freedom to let other people's actions move right past you. This is the freedom that allows you to see a traffic jam as an opportunity to listen to thirty minutes more of the Tony Robbins YouTube clip you just started.

Controlling what you can control gives you the power to change your mind-set. If you hold a door for someone, and they do not say thank you, that is out of your control. (I'll bet that this has happened to you, and when it did, you thought or whispered under your breath something not very nice. Or maybe you took it even further, and assumed that the person thought he was superior and deserved door-openers.) This is an example of letting other people affect your actions. It's also a hint that you need to examine your motive. Did you truly want to do something nice or do you require recognition of your "nice" actions?

The thing you must understand about only controlling what you can control is that the only person you have any control over is you. You have no idea what other people are going through, or what's driving their actions.

Now that you know this, let's re-visit the holding the door incident. You hold the door, and a lady walks through with a blank look and without saying a word. Now imagine you can see into people's lives like a sixth sense. Just as you are about to say something snarky, you realize that this lady just buried her eighteen-year-old son. Now you actually begin to empathize with her. As we know, a sixth sense is not going to happen, but the fact remains the same — everyone is dealing with something you know nothing about. Or, maybe they are just jerks. Either way, you can't control their actions, *you can only control your actions or reactions.*

I've spent a lot of time working hard on this with all of my clients because shaping this perception will allow them to let the negativity go. Or, like Jay-Z says, "Get, that dirt of your shoulders."

On my journey to be a paid speaker, I had family members who could not believe the decision I'd made. Some reached out to tell me, "Good luck. Everyone wants to get in that industry." Other friends remained skeptical until after I'd made it. I can remember vividly a conversation with a friend that went like this:

ME: "I've left coaching, and I am going to be a speaker and performance coach."

HIM: "You better be prepared to speak for a few years for free."

I laughed, because I'd already been paid $1,500 for an event. I shared this with him, but he was still certain it wasn't going to work. Three months later, I had nine paid performance-coaching clients and three more speaking gigs lined up. That means I went from $1,500 to more than $30,000 in my first three months. Needless to say, I stopped hearing about how it wouldn't work.

I have never let anyone tell me what was realistic or unrealistic, and I encourage you to take the same approach. I could have let my buddy get the best of me, I could have said, "You're probably right" … but there was no way I was going to start thinking like that. People will always tell you their thoughts, but it is your choice how you let those thoughts effect you.

Along your journey, you will encounter people and situations that will create adversity. Your ability to stay positive in these situations will completely depend on the work you put into the **mental game,** and you being able to recognize and replace negative thoughts. Keep the power of your future squarely in your mind because that will keep it squarely in your hands. The power of practiced positivity is undeniable, and it's overwhelming in a completely wonderful way.

HUSTLE 'TIL IT HAPPENS

Hustle 'Til It Happens is a statement that declares, **the only way your dream is going to work is by adding hard work to your mission.**

You can't just sit around, thinking or visualizing. You **must** take action. And, in most cases, you will need **massive action** in order to reach your dreams.

Hustle 'Til It Happens is about doing what needs to be done, when it needs to be done, regardless of the time, or what your friends are doing, or how much sleep you are losing. This is a call to action that says "Get up and take the necessary steps *with no regard to your current comfort level* to create a life that you already know is happening." This is the final step to process. This is the action that is going to help you run down your dreams and live a life of defined success.

Although this is about taking action, I want everyone to understand by "action," I don't mean "busy." Busy is horrible word — it's a word we use to make ourselves feel important. Busy shows a need for outside praise. Busy is not actually working — it's more *acting* than working. "Busy work" is work you add because you feel like you need to be doing something all the time.

STEP 22: HUSTLE 'TIL IT HAPPENS

Keep your focus on your process or on your daily list. Remember that this is a marathon — this is your whole life — and there will always be something to do. If you're adding tasks just to stay busy, stop. Only add tasks that bring value. Busy-ness brings stress and stress brings anxiety — and anxiety creates a negative mind. And as we now know, a negative mind creates inaction and avoidable failure.

Exercise:

Make your list (activities to do for a day) the night before, or in the morning before you start working. Why? To prioritize what needs to be done. Once you create your list and get it done, your day is done. You can now enjoy your free time. There is always more to do tomorrow, but we must live a full life if we're going to be productive on a consistent basis. I do this every day — sometimes I am done at 2 p.m., and sometimes I finish at 9 p.m. If I'm done early, I do things that I want to do for the rest of the day. Sometimes these things involve my work, but they can also be fun things like going on a boat, golfing, or even writing. Other times I visit with friends, go shopping, or simply relax and take in the day with a good book.

SAMPLE LIST OF THINGS I NEED TO DO ON CERTAIN DAYS:

Give Thanks

Send love

Workout

Check new Listings

Check expired listings

Check price changes

Send thank you letter to my appointment yesterday

Pick up closing gift

Meet with the team

LIVE YOUR DREAM

In your hands, you hold a tried and true program that has taken people from a negative or stagnant life of unfulfilled dreams to a life of intention. **Dream bold** and create your own unique goal — a goal that was once out of sight, but is now running straight toward you as if it wants to be caught.

Remember that there are no short cuts in life, especially in pursuit of your ultimate success. Of course, there are no guarantees either. This is not me copping out if you fail — this is me being honest. I failed to reach the big leagues due to situations outside my control, but through the **Hustle 'Til It Happens** program I developed along the way, I was able to pick myself back up and continue to pursue my defined success.

Now, you can too.

Go get your dreams!

Sam Flamont

P: 231-633-8326

E: samflamont@samflamont.com

Website: www.samflamont.com

Made in the USA
Columbia, SC
30 July 2021